Marketing Issues in Western Europe: Changes and Developments

Marketing Issues in Western Europe: Changes and Developments has been co-published simultaneously as *Journal of Euromarketing*, Volume 14, Numbers 1/2 2004.

T0300052

Marketing Issues in Western Europe: Changes and Developments

Erdener Kaynak, PhD, DSc
Frédéric Jallat, PhD
Editors

Marketing Issues in Western Europe: Changes and Developments
has been co-published simultaneously as *Journal of Euromarketing*,
Volume 14, Numbers 1/2 2004.

Routledge
Taylor & Francis Group
LONDON AND NEW YORK

First published by
International Business Press®, 10 Alice Street, Binghamton, NY 13904-1580 USA
International Business Press® is an imprint of The Haworth Press, Inc., 10 Alice Street, Binghamton, NY 13904-1580 USA.

This edition published 2012 by Routledge
2 Park Square, Milton Park, Abingdon, Oxon OX14 4RN
711 Third Avenue, New York, NY 10017, USA
Routledge is an imprint of the Taylor & Francis Group, an informa business

Marketing Issues in Western Europe: Changes and Developments has been co-published simultaneously as *Journal of Euromarketing*, Volume 14, Numbers 1/2 2004.

Cover design by Jennifer M. Gaska

Library of Congress Cataloging-in-Publication Data

Marketing issues in Western Europe : changes and developments / Erdener Kaynak, Frederic Jallat, editors.
    p. cm.
    "Marketing Issues in Western Europe: Changes and Developments has been co-published simultaneously as Journal of Euromarketing, volume 14, numbers 1/2 2004."
    Includes bibliographical references.

1. Marketing–Europe, Western. I. Kaynak, Erdener. II. Jallat, Frederic. III. Journal of Euro-marketing.

HF5415.12.E8M385 2005
381'.094–dc22

                      2004026734

ISBN-13: 978-0-7890-2837-2

Marketing Issues in Western Europe: Changes and Developments

CONTENTS

ABOUT THE EDITORS

Erdener Kaynak, PhD, DSc, is currently Professor of Marketing and Chair of the Marketing Program at the School of Business Administration of The Pennsylvania State University at Harrisburg. He holds a BSc degree from Istanbul University, an MA in Marketing from the University of Lancaster and a PhD in Marketing Management from Cranfield University in the United Kingdom and an Honorary DSc degree in Economics from Turku School of Economics and Business Administration, Finland. He has extensive teaching, research, consulting, and advisory experiences in five continents at over forty countries. A prolific writer, Dr. Kaynak has published 24 books; three of which were translated into Japanese, Hindi, and Chinese and over 200 articles in refereed scholarly and professional journals on international marketing, cross-national/cultural consumer behavior, marketing in the third world, and comparative marketing systems.

He served as a member of the Kyrgyz President's Task Force on Science and Education and has been heavily involved in the development, running, and improvement of the first Western style Business School in Kyrgyz Republic-Bishkek International Academy of Business and Management (BIABM), now re-named as Academy of Management during a period of five years. A frequent contributor to executive training programs around the globe, Dr. Kaynak has recently offered seminars before senior executives and public policy makers in such countries as Colombia, Peru, Canada, Finland, Norway, Estonia, Brazil, Turkey, Italy, Hong Kong, Australia, South Africa, The People's Republic of China, Kyrgyz Republic, The Sudan, Macau, Egypt, Sweden, Germany, Japan, Australia, Denmark and Thailand. Dr. Kaynak has also served as a business consultant, training adviser, and a seminar leader with a number of North/South American, European, and Asian companies and institutions. For the last eighteen years, Dr. Kaynak has been serving as the Executive Editor for International Business Press (IBP) as well as the Senior Editor (International Business) for The Haworth Press, Inc., of New York, London, and Victoria (AU). In this capacity, he serves as Founding Editor and Editor-in-Chief of six scholarly international marketing and business journals. Dr. Kaynak was the first Penn State University recipient of the J. William Fulbright Senior Specialist Scholar Fellowship.

Dr. Kaynak has contributed articles to such scholarly publications as *Journal of Advertising Research*, *Journal of the Academy of Marketing Science*, *Journal of Business Research*, *Management International Review*, *Industrial Marketing Management*, *Journal of World Business*, *International Marketing Review*, *Journal of Macromarketing*, *European Journal of Marketing*, and many others.

Frédéric Jallat, PhD, is currently Professor of Marketing and Academic Director of the graduate program in International Business and Projects Management at the European School of Management (ESCP-EAP) in Paris, France and Professor and Academic Director of the graduate program in Marketing at the Graduate School of Business (ESA) in Beirut, Lebanon. He received his Master degree from the University Panthéon-Sorbonne, France and a PhD degree in Management Sciences and Business Administration from University Aix-Marseille III and ESSEC, France. He has been a visiting faculty and a visiting professor in four continents at over twenty universities and research institutions including New York University, Stanford University, the University of Texas at Austin, the Asian Institute of Technology and the Foreign Trade Academy of Russia.

Professor Jallat has been the recipient of a number of research scholarships and distinctions, most notably: Research Fellow of the Center for International Business and Economic Growth, Rochester Institute of Technology, Research Fellow of the Italian Research Council, French Government Scholarship, Member of the Board of Country Directors, International Management Development Association, Member of the National Commission on Business Education and Training, French Ministry of Education. He received two International Education Grants and a Dissertation Research Grant from the French Foundation for Management Education and a PhD award from ESSEC.

Prior to his appointment at the European School of Management, Dr. Jallat has served as a business consultant and Academic Coordinator in Marketing for the undergraduate program in Economic and Social Sciences at the University Panthéon-Sorbonne, France.

Dr. Jallat serves as an editorial board member for the *Journal of Euromarketing* and the *Journal of Transnational Management Devel-*

opment, USA and *Revue Française du Marketing*, France. He serves also as a review board member for the *Journal of Product & Brand Management*, UK and *Revue Française de Gestion*, France. He is an author/co-author of fifteen books and book chapters and of over thirty ranked academic articles in a variety of journals around the world. Professor Jallat is a member of the scientific committee for the MBA programs at the European School of Management and a Professor in the doctoral program in Strategy at University Paris-Nanterre, France. His research focuses on Western European Business, Cross-Cultural Management and International Marketing.

Marketing in Western Europe: A Monolith or a Multidimensional Market?

Erdener Kaynak
Frédéric Jallat

SUMMARY. Europe is emerging as an important internal market. As such, it offers tremendous opportunities and challenges for companies wanting to explore trade and investment possibilities. It is pointed out that Europe is the largest regional market in the world where the highest trade takes place among the member states of the European Union. On May 1st, 2004, the European Union was enlarged to 25 member countries which now offer major opportunities for firms of all sizes providing products and services to the consumers of some 450 million people. In order to capitalize on these vast market and business opportunities, companies must fully understand the changing macro environmental and consumer/organizational buyer behavior trends and take appropriate actions. In this fast changing Euro market, increasingly more pro-active marketing approaches must be undertaken for the attainment of better results. *[Article copies available for a fee from The Haworth Document Delivery Service: 1-800-HAWORTH. E-mail address: <docdelivery@haworthpress.com>*

Erdener Kaynak is Professor of Marketing, Chair of the Marketing Program, School of Business Administration, Pennsylvania State University at Harrisburg, 777 West Harrisburg Pike, Middletown, PA 17057, USA (E-mail: k9x@psu.edu). Frédéric Jallat is Professor of Marketing, Paris Graduate School of Business, ESCP-EAP European School of Management, 79 avenue de la Republique, 75543 Paris Cedex 11, France (E-mail: jallat@escp-eap.net).

[Haworth co-indexing entry note]: "Marketing in Western Europe: A Monolith or a Multidimensional Market?" Kaynak, Erdener, and Frédéric Jallat. Co-published simultaneously in *Journal of Euromarketing* (International Business Press, an imprint of The Haworth Press, Inc.) Vol. 14, No. 1/2, 2004, pp. 1-14; and: *Marketing Issues in Western Europe: Changes and Developments* (eds: Erdener Kaynak, and Frédéric Jallat) International Business Press, an imprint of The Haworth Press, Inc., 2004, pp. 1-14. Single or multiple copies of this article are available for a fee from The Haworth Document Delivery Service [1-800-HAWORTH, 9:00 a.m. - 5:00 p.m. (EST). E-mail address: docdelivery@haworthpress.com].

1

KEYWORDS. Western Europe, marketing, single Europe, market characteristics, European enlargement

INTRODUCTION

Western Europe is not a mass, homogeneous market but comprises of markets of different sizes and importance. There are at least three sub-markets, namely; European Union countries (the number is 25 as of May 1st, 2004), European Free Trade Area countries (the number is 4), and the remaining accession countries of south eastern European countries (the number is 3). The feasibility of standardizing European marketing has often been questioned on the grounds of economic, cultural, and behavioral divergences among European consumers of 450 million now. Hence, it is extremely difficult to talk about pan-European marketing in the foreseeable future (Diamantopoulos 1995). Understanding marketing systems, marketing practices of companies and/or industries as well as consumer markets in this significant market is very critical. Though the economies of the region and countries therein possess high growth potential, they simultaneously pose special challenges and opportunities to global marketers.

EUROPEAN MARKET CHARACTERISTICS

The subject of western European marketing is a difficult and complex one. Indeed, specialists who attempt to come to terms with the specifics of a European approach to marketing are generally required to bear in mind certain crucial points:

1. If one considers, as have many cross-cultural and political experts, that the complexity of a European continent is defined by a combination of its diversity and density, it is clear that western Europe stands apart from other regions of the world that are characterized by either high densities and homogeneous populations (e.g., Japan and Oriental China) or low densities and heterogeneous populations (e.g., North America). In fact, in terms of phys-

ical geography, Europe covers only 10 million square kilometres (6.3 million square miles), representing one-fifth of the Eurasian continent. Within that geographical area–which is very comparable to the US territory in term of size–various ethnic groups speak more than 20 different languages, five main religions are widely represented, and major differences in economic development, social organization, and legal and political systems serve more to fragment the continent than to unite it. Europe today has more people and a larger combined GNP than the USA. It represents one of the most potentially lucrative markets in the world. There is a European Union, but there is no such thing as a "European." The region is highly diverse in terms of geography, language, economic development, spending habits, disposable income. Europe's population is fairly well dispersed with Germany making up 22% of the population, France, United Kingdom and Italy each with 16%, Spain 11%, and the remainder of the continent 19% (Hengst 2000).

It is obviously clear that the research approach and selection of topical areas vary according to the specific European marketing management context in which the research is undertaken. As a result, the diversity and complexity of the European continent leads us to speak of different approaches to marketing in Europe as opposed to a single western European marketing approach. This is the reason why the contributions presented in this issue are favoring as much inter-European comparisons in marketing practices and strategies as comparisons between Western European States and the rest of the world.

2. Without detailing the exchange organization or the competing policies within the European Union, and in spite of German, French or Italian economic power, the British model today represents one of the most frequently used styles of thought on the continent. American management models, derived from British economic theories of the 18th century and the country's mercantile and liberal tradition, are favorably accepted in the northern and northwest regions of the continent. In fact, it even has been observed that the differences between the United Kingdom and the United States, from a marketing point of view, often seem to be less significant than those distinguished between different European countries. In reality, it is less the technical analysis or newly emergent concepts that enabled European marketing to dif-

ferentiate itself than the different ways of appreciating events in companies. This European approach often diverges from the American vision of business life, which places great emphasis on the role of the economic environment in the life of the state, its citizens and workers. Business life in Europe is indeed influenced by a variety of political and social preoccupations:

More often faced with cultural diversity, turbulent environments, economic problems, and market fragmentation–and probably also less orthodox than their American counterparts–the strategic "great precepts" derived from traditional neo-classical theories are progressively being replaced in Europe by more multi-varied strategies for competition, ones that take into account the specifics of the organization and the instabilities of the economic and social environments. With its many internal tensions and abrupt turnabouts, Europe has learned to manage its diversity and respond to the obstacles it faces. Throughout history, Europe has been able to retain its multitude of cultures, varied social organizations, distinct forms of expression, and disparate modes of thought. This has clearly influenced the way many Europeans think about globalization: the taking into account of the diversity of their markets, of their individual characteristics, and the integration of historical, political, and cultural information in management policies. These forces confer a vital addition to European marketing policies. In some countries, such as Germany, France or Sweden, the legal principles of competition and consumption are distinct and separate elements. This is because the customer is not automatically recognized as "an independent, responsible and autonomous arbitrator," as is the case in the United States.

Even if these arguments can be discussed, the European legislator has legalized his decision by evoking the protection of both the customer and equitable competition.

Economic crisis and the European integration policy have had major repercussions on the lives of European citizens since the mid-80s, and have contributed to reinforce the role of the state in business life. One has seen the development of stronger bonds between political and business circles, the orientation of industry at a national level, major national projects, diverse tariffs, etc. Although employment rates have been somewhat variable during the past two decades, the level of unemployment in many EU nations remains high compared to the US. Contrary to the widely-envied, but closely watched, American economic model, continental Europe often prefers a political vision, more collective and less liberal in nature. In spite of objections often voiced by tax payers, European citizens would be satisfied by industrial policies of total employment and equitable payments by their governments. In this context, the company's vocation is not completely financial and oriented by profit, nor is the mission of its management solely linked to performance. A form of capitalism that involves employees enhances their negotiating power in the company and helps to integrate the organization within its environment.

3. Another aspect of the European marketing process is the continuous monitoring of environmental factors that may affect future marketing strategy in Europe. A new environment for marketing is being established in Europe as a result of changing business, cultural, economic, and political relationships. It was pointed out by Savitt (1998) that European markets are taking on new dimensions that defy recognized geographical, political and cultural boundaries. He recommends understanding the differences among European markets before trying to discover elements of commonality. Although hundreds of legislations and directives issued and enacted by the European Parliament must fully be considered in the development and implementation of marketing strategies, policies and plans, a more proactive approach will be needed for better planning. This approach will necessitate consideration of the broader social, cultural, and legal-political systems of the countries of Western Europe. An advanced environmental analysis system is needed to anticipate and manage issues beyond legal compliance (LeClair 2000).

In short, what we find relative to European marketing is that it is more the case that the vocabulary, the information sources, the large consulting firms, and the literature of the field have been imported than the entirety of the social practices and meanings they represent. Although a certain degree of convergence is occurring due to developments in macro-economies and the EU, it remains too early to talk about a unified set of European marketing theories. A consideration of the subject still requires the researcher to take a "tour" of Europe. Despite the fact that specialists tend to agree that cultural variables should not be overestimated in their attempts to explain marketing phenomena, it also should be clear that the areas of research chosen and the orientations taken by researchers within a country provide insight into that country's character, history, and values.

IS EUROPE A MONOLITH OR DIVERGENT MARKET?

With the emergence of globalization and the progressive evolution of a single European market as undeniable facts of life, marketers have begun to rethink the implications of these developments for their research and applied activities. While it may be overly pessimistic to presume that a single European marketing approach is not possible, in our view, marketers, at least in the foreseeable future, must continue to approach the European marketplace with full awareness of European diversity. Our admittedly limited "tour of Europe" has revealed how marketing approaches are firmly embedded in the history, values, national character, cognitive styles, and other contextual factors of specific European nations. These influencing factors shape not only marketing strategies, but the research approaches and selection of topical areas that underlie those strategies. In a study of the marketing strategies and headquarters-subsidiary relationship of German and French subsidiaries operating in the United Kingdom, German companies were found to pursue market-focused strategies with an emphasis on product quality. Their French counterparts adopted a more short-term orientation with a stronger emphasis on cost-related strategies (Shaw 2001).

Our main objective in this special volume is to analyze the European specifics that influence certain aspects of marketing and to consider some areas of research that clearly illustrate the European marketing diversity. Some of most critical issues related to western European marketing may be outlined as follows:

1. Legally, Europe is a single market, but it is not a mass (monolith) market, but a culturally and linguistically diverse market with a number of divergent, sub-markets.
2. There are regional, country, and in-country differences within the market. The differences between the north and the south versus east and west are enormous indeed. As well, there are discernable differences between Greece and the United Kingdom, Portugal versus Denmark, Italy versus Sweden, Ireland versus Austria. Tastes vary from country to country–sometimes dramatically–and marketing planning should be done on a local, not a pan-European, level.
3. Within country differences necessitate different marketing practices, as well. In the United Kingdom, there are vast purchasing and consumption, level of economic development differences among England, Scotland, Wales and Northern Ireland. The same

idea applies to Greece and Italy, where there are vast differences between northern and southern parts of these countries. The look and feel of your product must work within the cultural context of the individual European country. As an example, Germans tend to like to see benefits listed, but you are less likely to see side-by-side comparisons, as you will see in the USA. The Spanish prefer a more emotional touch and fewer facts.

4. There are also in-country regional differences in the way of consumption, buying behaviour, and purchasing. A case example is England, where there are vast differences between northern England (Yorkshire or Lancashire) and southern part of England (Carnwall).

5. Except the three monarchies (United Kingdom, Denmark and Sweden), twelve others are part of the Euro-zone.

6. Unified Europe has created convergence on the part of the supply side of the equation which was achieved through hundreds of legislation enacted through the European Parliament. But, vast differences in demand still prevail among the member countries which will continue for a long time to come.

7. Business is becoming much more international or multinational in Europe. British, Dutch, and German retailers operate conveniently in a multiple European environments and, in spite of some local difficulties, are succeeding (Savitt 1998).

Ten years ago there was considerable discussion of "pan-European" marketing in response to the Single European Market. The article by Halliburton and Hünerberg reviews the strategic marketing issues facing enlarged Europe today. Based upon the core issue of segmentation, it outlines a countervailing set of drivers towards and against European convergence, and proposes a European marketing convergence framework. Evidence is found for increasing European convergence. The article then examines the implications for marketing decisions and outlines some of the resulting strategic marketing options.

Over the ten-year period since the symbolic SEM date of 1993, pan-European marketing appears to be an emerging reality and companies with more or less standardized European marketing approaches already exist. Companies must therefore find ways to reconcile simultaneously the advantages of pan-European scale with increasing customer demand for choice and persistent differences in national or regional consumer preferences. They will therefore need to be much better informed as to social and technology trends within Europe, to the new media and emerging distribution channels. They must develop new ways to handle trans-national customer relationships and to exploit the benefits of European one-to-one marketing. They will need to adopt new organizational solutions, management styles and new sources of information in Europe. They will need: to establish which countries or parts of countries are inherently interesting; to discover whether cross-border segments with similar demand criteria are sufficiently significant; to establish suitable market accessibility through distribution and media channels; and to decide which marketing instruments can be standardized over which segments, and to which extent.

After ten years, many of the hundreds of directives envisaged by the founding members of the European Union are now in place. Prior to and since the formation of the EU internal market, past research and scholarly articles have speculated on changes in marketing, business, and economic conditions that would likely result. But, from an international marketing perspective, what has the EU internal market really achieved over the past decade? The study by Sciglimpaglia and Saghafi addresses the marketing impact of the European single market formation from the perspective of the European corporate managers. The principal objectives were to highlight the impacts of the creation of the internal market on strategic marketing decisions, compared to pre-EU conditions, the harmonization of marketing programs, and the effectiveness and efficiency of post-unification of marketing.

The present study used on an on-line survey that addressed major issues structured around product strategy, promotion, distribution, and pricing. The results are based on an executive survey of nearly 100 corporate respondents in the EU, with the majority located in the UK or in Germany. Roughly three-quarters represent European companies, with the remainder mainly representing American firms located in Europe. These respondents currently serve as top level executives or directors, department heads, or middle managers. The major areas of responsibility of these executives are sales or marketing management, international operations, and corporate planning. The majority of these respondents represent large firms with 5,000 or more employees, with the firms occupying a wide array of industries and range of consumer and business markets.

Many of the findings of the study follow predictions of possible marketing strategy changes as a function of the formation of the internal market. Results show that product strategy, in particular, appears to have been greatly impacted by the formation of the internal market. This is seen in general agreement among respondents regarding increased product availability and variety, widespread use of Euro branding and improvements in overall product quality. Furthermore, as expected, the creation of a single market is viewed as having led to more centralized manufacturing, leading to scale economies and efficiency in production. Advertising and promotion practices are seen as having moved significantly towards more integration and standardization, spurred by changes in media use and tactics. Distribution strategy is seen to have benefited greatly from the single market. In general, pan-European retailing is seen as having led to more centralized manufacturing, leading to scale economies and efficiency in production. Advertising and promotion practices are seen as having moved significantly towards more integration and standardization, spurred by changes in media use and tactics. Distribution strategy is seen to have benefited greatly from the single market. In general, pan-European retailing is seen as having gained dominance, with smaller retailers eliminated or absorbed and with wholesalers having become larger and more powerful, through mergers, acquisitions or alliances. In contrast, views on pricing were somewhat surprising. Price harmonization is, as expected, taking place faster in the industrial sector and, overall, the prices of manufactured goods are seen as having become more harmonized than those of services. However, the executives surveyed do not generally agree that increased competition has led to a general trend towards lower prices, especially when production efficiencies are achieved. Furthermore, it is suggested that the single market creation and the successful introduction of euro has not succeeded in making EU companies more price competitive.

The paper by Palmer and Pels presents exploratory research that investigates the linkages between market orientation, contemporary marketing practice and performance outcomes. Comparative data is presented from Argentina and the UK. This is the first time that work of this nature, comparing developed and emerging economies in varying conditions of environmental turbulence, has been conducted.

Market orientation is considered as a component of superior performance and numerous studies have been conducted using research instruments developed primarily by Kohli and Jaworski (1990), Narver and Slater (1990), and also others. An influential study by Matsuno and Mentzer (2000) developed this further by considering business strategy as an intermediate variable between market orientation and corporate performance.

The Contemporary Marketing Practice (CMP) group, an international group of marketing academics, has developed a framework that gives insight into how marketing is currently conducted (Coviello,

Brodie, Danaher and Johnston 2002). The paper proposes that generic measures of strategy implementation and corporate performance are at too high a level of abstraction and that more sensitive measures are necessary to give greater insight. Building on the work of Matsuno and Mentzer (2000), this research applies the CMP framework and considers marketing outcomes as measures of performance in order that better explanations can be uncovered.

Business takes place within the wider environmental context and, in line with identified research gaps (Kohli, Jaworski and Kumar 1993, Selnes, Jaworski and Kohli 1996) and consistent with other work in this area (Olsen 2001), the study was positioned within the context of Argentina, an emerging economy experiencing environmental turbulence, and the UK, a developed, stable economy.

The approach is revelatory and inductive, seeking to build theory and uncover new insights and understanding by the use of a realist epistemology. Whilst the data has limitations, the research has enabled the development of a theoretical model and a series of propositions that form the basis for further, confirmatory work.

A vast number of authors in consumer behavior and marketing psychology have studied the issue of why consumers choose or prefer one product to the other. Studies can be found addressing both the comparisons between domestic products as well as situations where domestic products were chosen over foreign products or vice versa. While most–if not all–of the domestic-domestic constructs have also been applied in studies that focused on preference and choice processes in domestic-foreign situations, no study could be found that used the opposite approach, that is, attempting to explain domestic-domestic choice processes with a construct originally generated from the research in domestic-foreign situations. It is intuitively, logically, and empirically reasonable to argue that as long as domestic-domestic variables are sufficient to explain phenomena in domestic choice situations, the use of other constructs is unnecessary. However, by investigating the intra-German market which exhibits a struggle between Neue Länder (former East Germany) and Alte Länder (former West Germany) products, the paper by Wolfgang Hinck argues that the application of selected foreign-domestic constructs may provide a better explanation for phenomena in specific domestic-domestic situations. The paper coins the term "domestic animosity," a term describing near-hostile feelings among citizens of one nation. To test the hypothesis of an effect of domestic animosity on purchasing willingness, Klein et al.'s (1998) *foreign* animosity construct was used. Using data collected at two points in time, the results show that the effect of domestic animosity on willingness to buy Alte Länder products is even stronger than the effect of animosity in previous *cross*-national studies. The results confirm that animosity, in fact, is a construct that does not just explain international phenomena, but can also help explain domestic situations. It is suggested that the same experience could currently affect firms in almost every nation of the world. For marketing managers all over the globe, therefore, it is recommended to carefully investigate the chances of an occurrence of domestic animosity in their home markets.

Managers face many challenges to achieve and sustain high business performance. One way to achieve this in turbulent and rapidly changing markets is through building and deploying effective boundary spanning capabilities such as nurturing strategic alliances, creating networks, and building effective relationships with customers, partners, and suppliers. Using a resource-based perspective, Tsarenko et al. investigate the impact of customer orientation and employee orientation profiles on a business's portfolio of boundary spanning capabilities. The paper reports results of a study conducted across two continents, Europe (focused on the UK) and Australasia (focused on Australia).

The results show a high degree of consistency across the two countries studied. With regard to three sets of boundary spanning capabilities (strategic alliances, networking and relationship management), similar relationships were found with a high but balanced focus on both customers and employees yielding the highest level of capability. Surprisingly, however, in neither country was supply chain capability found to be related to focus on either. Inside-out, or internal support capabilities, were found to be less dependent on employee focus than anticipated.

The study found that employee focus and customer focus are both important to the generation of boundary spanning capabilities in both the UK and Australia. Where both customer focus and employee focus were high, however, it was found that there was a greater effect on capability in Australia than in the UK. This may reflect the geographic dispersion of the Australasian market, together with the greater dependence of Australian companies on foreign markets, necessitating heightened boundary spanning capability. As the European market expands with the accession of ten further states in May of 2004, we might anticipate that boundary spanning capability will become even more significant in European markets.

Both customer orientation and employee orientation are important and need investment to help firms cope with environmental dynamics and manage the organization-environment interface. In an ideal world, firms should pursue both, but where scarce resources necessitate a trade-off, the evidence from this study suggests that greater emphasis on customer-orientation is most effective in creating boundary spanning capability.

Dumping is present in the European Union market when the export price at which a product is sold in the Community market is shown to be lower than what is considered "normal value." While in most cases, the normal value is calculated as the price in the exporter's home market, the normal value, in the case of China, is the home market price in a so-called analogue country. The philosophy behind using an analogue country when calculating the normal value is based on the belief that intervention by the Chinese government in price setting, etc., distorts home market prices, making them unusable in normal value calculations. Because of the ongoing reforms in China, which have led to an increasing number of Chinese companies operating on market economy principles, Chinese companies have, since 1 July 1998, been allowed to apply for individual market economy status and in such cases, the normal value of a product is based on the home market price of the company. The criterion which the companies have to fulfil is that there must not be any significant external interference in their economic decision-making in relation to prices, costs, investments, etc.

Based on the practice of the EU anti-dumping policy against China in 1990-2001, the paper by Jørgen Ulff-Møller Nielsen shows that companies operating in China and exporting to or planning to export to the EU market have a number of possibilities for lessening the threat of or the size of EU anti-dumping measures. Firstly, the companies may use the information given by the EU institutions in relation to anti-dumping cases. This information may be useful for Chinese companies in formulating their price strategies on the EU market. Secondly, since the treatment of a Chinese company depends on the strength of its links to Chinese public authorities, such dependency should be reduced. There are numerous ways of doing this. A state-owned Chinese company may try to become privatised or may enter into a joint venture with a foreign company, thus ensuring that the joint venture obtains an export license and the right to sell on the Chinese domestic market. The combination of such rights and application for market economy status or at least individual treatment, opens the possibility of a reduced level of duty. By entering into negotiations with the EU, the Chinese company may also have the possibility of obtaining permission to convert a duty into a price agreement, resulting in better economic performance. A foreign company investing in China should prefer a wholly owned company or should at least acquire majority ownership.

The Chinese membership of the WTO gives Chinese companies an opportunity to check the legality of the EU anti-dumping decisions by using the dispute settlement system of the WTO. In addition, instead of just having the possibility of applying for "market economy status" and waiting for approval or rejection, the Chinese producers have a WTO-based legal right to "market economy status" if market economy conditions obviously obtain.

Past research in cross-cultural advertising has focused on the facets of cultural variations of individualism-collectivism and uncertainty avoidance. Especially, the second one has been conceptualized as the extent to which a culture is anxious about uncertain situations and therefore establishes structure to avoid experiencing this continuous threat. The dimensions of uncertainty avoidance seems particularly relevant to the study of fear appeals owing to its association with an increased need for security. Hence, an understanding of cultural differences is essential to communicate effectively to consumers from different cultural backgrounds. The purpose of the study by Vincent and Dubinsky is to examine the influence of culture on fear by using the protection motivation model as a basic theoretical framework. In their study, France and the USA were chosen as target countries to represent opposite ends of the uncertainty avoidance continuum. Study results indicated that compared to a low level of threat, a high level induces greater fear and leads to a higher likelihood of purchasing the advertised product. No significant differences on fear were found between French and US subjects.

CONCLUSIONS

It is observed that the European markets are in a stage of rapid growth and development. This trend is expected to grow at an accelerating rate in the future. The changing macro environmental and consumer behaviour trends will have major implications for the marketing strategies of firms operating in the region. Substantial differences in the economic, cultural, and infrastructural environments still exist in Europe. Despite these divergences, blending of lifestyles and growing uniformity in consumer tastes and purchasing behaviour will progressively minimize the importance of traditional geographical and political boundaries within Europe.

REFERENCES

Diamantopoulos, A; B.B. Schlegelmilch; and J.P. Du Preez (1995), "Lessons for Pan-European Marketing? The Role of Consumer Preferences in Fine Tuning the Product-Market Fit," *International Marketing Review*, Vol. 12, No. 2, pp. 38-52.

Hengst, Rainer (2000), "Plotting Your Global Strategy," *Direct Marketing*, Vol. 63, No. 4, (August), pp. 52-57.

Jallat F., Kimmel A. (2002), "Marketing in Culturally Diverse Environments: The Case of Western Europe," *Business Horizons*, Vol. 45, No. 4, July-August 2002, pp. 30-36.

LeClair, Debbie Thorne (2000), "Marketing Planning and the Policy Environment in the European Union," *International Marketing Review*, Vol. 17, No. 3, pp. 193-207.

Savitt, Ronald (1998), "This Thing I Call Europe," *International Marketing Review*, Vol. 15, No. 6, pp. 444-447.

Shaw, Vivienne Topajka (2001), "The Marketing Strategies of French and German Companies in the U.K.," *International Marketing Review*, Vol. 18, No. 6, pp. 611-632.

Pan-European Marketing
Ten Years After 1993–
A Current Appraisal
and Proposed Conceptual Framework

Chris Halliburton
Reinhard Hünerberg

SUMMARY. Ten years ago there was considerable discussion of "pan-European" marketing in response to the Single European Market. This article reviews the strategic marketing issues facing Europe today. Based upon the core issue of segmentation, it outlines a countervailing set of drivers towards and against European convergence, and proposes a European marketing convergence framework. Evidence is found for increasing European convergence. The article then examines the implications for marketing decisions and outlines some of the resulting strategic marketing

Chris Halliburton is Professor of International Marketing and UK Director at ESCP-EAP, European School of Management, Oxford, England. Reinhard Hünerberg is Professor of Marketing, University of Kassel, Germany.

Address correspondence to: Professor C. Halliburton, 12 Merton Street, Oxford OX1 4JH, England (E-mail: challibu@escp-eap.net), or to Professor R. Hünerberg, Uni-Kassel, FG Marketing, Diagonale 12, D-34127 Kassel, Germany (E-mail: huenerberg@wirtschaft.uni-kassel.de).

[Haworth co-indexing entry note]: "Pan-European Marketing Ten Years After 1993–A Current Appraisal and Proposed Conceptual Framework." Halliburton, Chris, and Reinhard Hünerberg. Co-published simultaneously in *Journal of Euromarketing* (International Business Press, an imprint of The Haworth Press, Inc.) Vol. 14, No. 1/2, 2004, pp. 15-34; and: *Marketing Issues in Western Europe: Changes and Developments* (eds: Erdener Kaynak, and Frédéric Jallat) International Business Press, an imprint of The Haworth Press, Inc., 2004, pp. 15-34. Single or multiple copies of this article are available for a fee from The Haworth Document Delivery Service [1-800-HAWORTH, 9:00 a.m. - 5:00 p.m. (EST). E-mail address: docdelivery@haworthpress.com].

options. Over the ten-year period since the symbolic SEM date of 1993, pan-European marketing appears to be an emerging reality. *[Article copies available for a fee from The Haworth Document Delivery Service: 1-800-HAWORTH. E-mail address: <docdelivery@haworthpress.com> Website: <http://www.HaworthPress. com>* © *2004 by The Haworth Press, Inc. All rights reserved.]*

KEYWORDS. Pan-European marketing, European strategic marketing options, European marketing convergence, segmentation

BACKGROUND

Ten years ago, there was considerable discussion as to the emergence of "pan-European" marketing in response to the Single European Market (SEM). The "global versus local" debate, characterized by the classic dispute between Levitt and Kotler (Levitt, 1983 and Kotler, 1984), had polarized the issue. The practical challenge was less whether to 'go pan-European' but rather for which product/markets, with which aspects of marketing operations, and to which extent.

The beginning of 1993 was intended to be one of the milestones of European development, the Maastricht treaty of 1992 having transformed the European Community (EC) into the European Union (EU) and the end of 1992 marking the transition period towards the completion of the SEM. Since then major changes have taken place. Politically, the EU was enlarged from twelve to fifteen member states, incorporating some of the former EFTA countries, and starting from May 2004, embracing ten former Central and Eastern European states, most of them from the former communist world. Economically, there have been continued reforms, notably the introduction of a common currency, the Euro, in most of the original EC countries. Legally, there has been an increasing application of EU legislation, harmonization and industry de-regulation in most sectors, encouraging a pan-European strategy. As a result, pan-European competition has advanced, with a series of major mergers, acquisitions and alliances. Finally, Europe-wide market access has developed–this was a major constraint to pan-European marketing ten years ago, with predominantly national distribution channels and media. However, a number of major obstacles to integration such as deep-rooted consumer preferences, incomplete harmonization, continuing national subsidies, and tax differences still persist. The efforts to create a European constitution and to achieve fundamental reforms may not be implemented in an adequate way. Heterogeneity will definitely grow within a union of 25 nations. Enthusiasm to create the United States of Europe is constantly diminishing and concerns about the whole European project tend to prevail. Even the new member states' populations did not overwhelmingly welcome entry into the European Union.

One other major factor has been the development of the Internet, both as a new "business model" as well as a major communication medium further encouraging a global approach. The same is true for the advances in mobile communications. Early proponents of the so-called "New Economy" would have argued against the case for any specifically European marketing approach at all, in this new borderless world. The challenge now is to distinguish such Internet "hype" from the real impact of new technologies upon a pan-European approach, allowing Europe-wide access to consumer segments and on-line business relationships within specific industry sectors?

The question now, therefore, has to be asked whether pan-European marketing is still appropriate. It is no longer a question of myth or reality but of relevance or irrelevance. Does Europe really matter? How should appropriate pan-European marketing strategies, operations and processes be implemented? The purpose of this article is to review the strategic marketing issues in today's Europe, to propose a possible framework for analysis, and to outline some of the managerial implications of these developments.

SEGMENTATION–THE CORE ISSUE

"Pan-European" marketing means literally viewing Europe as a distinct geographic segment to be treated in a uniform way within Europe, but differently from other geographic regions. The central concept is therefore segmentation, using national borders as the criterion. Global marketing treats the world as one segment while multinational marketing sees the world as distinct country product/markets. Factors supporting the global view can be reduced to two complementary arguments–customer convergence ("the global (or Euro) consumer") and global product efficiencies ("the global (or Euro) product"). Proponents of the global view would imply that the European "question" is either irrelevant or, at best, transition from a national to a global approach.

The first question is whether segments of major importance can still be defined along borderlines of the single states within Europe. If this is the case, then Europe is too heterogeneous to treat as one large segment. To test this proposition, the researcher should define potential segments on the basis of non-geographical cluster variables and examine the extent to which the segments in question are significantly independent of specific countries (Hofstede, Steenkamp and Wedel, 1999). For example, a study of a major consumer product multinational looked at consumer usage/attitude behavior across countries resulting in a switch from 17 different national marketing programs in favor of 4 Euro-regions cutting across national boundaries (Halliburton and Hünerberg, 1993b).

The second question concerns the trans-European character of the segments. If there are identical segments in other parts of the world, then there is no European specificity. Thus, segments should also be analyzed to establish the extent to which they can be categorized by their European exclusivity. European automobile distribution illustrates this issue. There are numerous differences between distribution channels in the different countries, such as size, buildings, technical equipment and staff resulting from different national practices and legislation, as well as a number of similarities with countries outside Europe. However there is a common set of rules specific to the EU, the motor vehicle block exemption regulation, which governs the formulation of contracts between manufacturers and dealers (Commission Regulation (EC) No., 1400/2002 (2002)). Many marketing activities are not allowed, according to the new rules of 2002, for example, the obligation for dealers to offer only the manufacturer's original spare parts. If an automobile manufacturer wants to re-design his distribution network, the decision is to a large extent EU-driven and may be seen as having a European segmentation basis in clear distinction to other parts of the world.

Thirdly, a major prerequisite for any European segmentation is the definition of Europe. Increasingly, due to its constant enlargement, the continent of Europe is becoming more congruent with the European Union. The few exclusions, Switzerland and Norway and most of former Yugoslavia and Albania, are relatively small markets and may well be integrated in the future. The cases of states such as Bulgaria and Romania scheduled to join in 2007, and Ukraine, Belarus and Moldavia may be considered as less relevant because they are situated at the extreme periphery of Europe. Turkey is a rather special case because of its size and geographically spanning both Europe and Asia, it has long had an association with the EU, being its first Associate Member in 1964.

However, even if only the 25 members of 2004 are taken into account, the differences of relative income, consumption patterns, local tastes, linguistic and cultural factors remain in many respects (Jallat and Kimmel, 2002). Thus the requirement of homogeneity will often not be met if Euro-segments are formulated on this basis. On economic grounds there are in principle two "peripheral" sub-regions, the Mediterranean South and the new East. But not only is wealth distributed unevenly over the EU member states, there are also differing regional disparities within the countries, for example, between Italy's South and North or Germany's West and East. In addition similar segments, although not fully "pan-European," may exist crossing national borders, to form sub-European regions, for example, the Aachen-Maastricht-Liège region. Hence, the definition of a Pan-European approach can be a rather relative concept.

The attempt to impose a universal Pan-European solution upon all products is clearly misguided. Even within the same industry sector, pan-European and national or regional segments markets co-exist. For example, in the beer market there are few "Euro-products," such as Heineken lager or premium specialty beers, and in Germany there are over 1,000 individual brewers. Attempts to overstandardize can be as damaging in the face of real European differences as can the failure to capture scale economies if such national differences are only superficial. Figure 1 illustrates a countervailing set of convergence "drivers," simultaneously driving European, or global, convergence in opposition to trends towards divergence or fragmentation within Europe.

FIGURE 1. Convergence Drivers

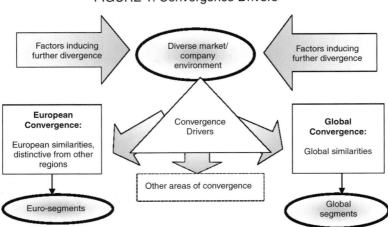

DRIVERS OF EUROPEAN CONVERGENCE/DIVERGENCE

In this section, we outline some of the convergence and divergence factors supporting the emergence of European segments. Figure 2 illustrates three such factors.

Collective identity reflects the fact that all European countries share more than two thousand years of relationships, categorized not only by wars, treaties and revolutions, but also by the exchange of goods and innovative ideas (Karklins, 2001). Trade relations and political links arguably have led to a form of shared, transnational identity, resulting from this common history, especially when viewed from outside of Europe (Altmann, 2001).

On the other hand, many European citizens seem to have partly lost their enthusiasm for the project because of bureaucracy, insufficient results, fear of losing national or regional identity, and poor marketing of the EU by its representatives. This skepticism also prevails in the new member states following the initial "back into Europe" enthusiasm in response to the collapse of communism (Haller, 1999).

There are three major areas in which this collective identity has been expressed in the more recent past–*economic, political* and *socio-cultural* factors (Jansen, 1999).

Economic convergence was the initial purpose of the European Union. The Treaty of Rome set out in Article 14/2 the realization of the so-called four freedoms (free movement of goods, capital, services, and persons). Since that time, we have seen: the Common Agricultural Policy (1962); the abolition of customs duties and introduction of a Common Customs Tariff vis-à-vis third countries (1968); the introduction of

FIGURE 2. Hierarchy of Drivers

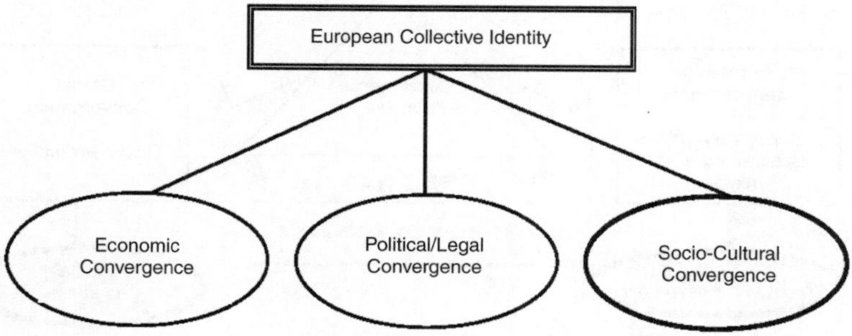

the European Monetary System with the ECU as single artificial currency and an Exchange Rate Mechanism to guarantee fixed but adjustable exchange rates (1979), being replaced by the Economic and Monetary Union and its single currency, the Euro (1999/2002); the Single Market Program, with the symbolic completion date of 1st January 1993, and with around 90% of the then envisaged 282 Directives and Regulations dealing with such matters as transportation and telecoms since passed by the Council of Ministers and with 80% of them implemented in the member states.

Financial schemes are to a large extent connected with EU program. There are four Structural Funds (European Agricultural Guidance and Guarantee Fund, Financial Instrument for Fisheries Guidance, European Regional Development Fund, European Social Fund) and numerous action programs and projects, e.g., the "Sixth Framework Program" to support the European Research Area, the "TEN-T" to develop the trans-European transport network, the "eTEN" to help the deployment of telecommunication networks based services, "Culture 2000" to promote a common cultural area, "Socrates" comprising eight different actions to Europeanize education or "Leonardo da Vinci" for transnational vocational training programs. Further evidence of the special coherence within the EU is the fact that in 1999, 63.5% of all EU (15) exports were intra-EU (EUROSTAT 2002, table 4c1ba), despite the fact that there is a multiple of six between intra-trade in the countries and cross-border trade, leaving still much room for further homogenization (Ghemawat, 2003, p. 141).

There are many indicators of increasing economic European conformity. From the fifteen EU member states, per capita GDP in 1992 showed Denmark leading, 2.28 times ahead of Spain, 3.43 times ahead of Greece and 4.54 times ahead of Portugal. By 2001, these differences have narrowed to 2.15, 2.84 and 2.96, respectively (OECD, from NTC, 1993 and 2002).

The result of the efforts to promote European economic coherence are a few unified, but highly regulated markets, especially European agriculture, several times reformed and heavily criticized for its excessive cost. Other industrial areas, such as energy or transport, are primarily subject to the Single Market program with resulting Europe-wide competition. However, there are still industries where national regulations apply, such as Defense and Pharmaceuticals.

This European economic convergence has so far gone well beyond that found in other regions or at a global level. Regional agreements such as NAFTA, ASEAN and Mercosur remain primarily at the level of free trade and customs union approaches. The 1995 transformation of GATT into the WTO and its enlargement, especially the admission of China, has to be seen as real global achievement, but does not approach the level of integration within Europe, producing arguably a greater set of both challenges and opportunities.

Political convergence is much less developed, although many economic aspects are interconnected with politics, for example taxation issues.

On domestic policy, "freedom, security and justice" now contains areas such as asylum policy, external border policy, immigration policy, and judicial co-operation in civil and criminal matters, police and customs co-operation. A cornerstone, not yet totally applied by all member states, is the Schengen agreement to abolish border controls within the EU.

Foreign and security policy is a more sensitive issue, as the Iraq war showed, although it was officially decided to develop a common policy in this field, too, when the treaty of Maastricht was signed. A Constitution for Europe could become a breakthrough not only for foreign European policy but still more so for European identity (Emmanouilidis and Giering, 2003).

Socio-cultural convergence has been encouraged by a number of EU initiatives. The Maastricht Treaty introduced culture into the policy fields of the EU, amended in the Amsterdam Treaty of 1997 (Article 151). Although the main objective was to support the diversity of European cultures, this may also encourage a sense of a common heritage. In addition, EU research policy, based on the launch of a European Research Area in 2000, and the approaches towards common employment and social policy guidelines can be seen as convergence enhancers.

The European Space for Higher Education, which started with the 1999 Bologna Declaration, intends to promote convergence of higher education systems and goes beyond present EU borders, with 29 signatory states to date. If this common project is realized by 2010 as planned, it may strongly influence the mobility of students and graduates and perhaps contribute more to European coherence than many other initiatives.

Regarding European consumer behavior, numerous studies have commented upon convergence tendencies (Hofstede, Wedel and Steenkamp, 2002; Grein, 2000; Lewis and Vickerstaff, 2001; Pasco, 2001; Savitt, 1998). Leeflang and van Raaij (1995) cite the growing percentage of older people, the decreasing size of households, the increasing number of immigrants (and their descendants), greater environmental and health concerns and growing consumption of services relative to durable consumption.

Infrastructure is crucial for all sectors described so far. Pan-European marketing presupposes the availability of cross-border means of information and communication as well as physical transport. Internet penetration, although lagging the USA, has been rapidly catching up, albeit with significant differences between countries–in 2001, 74% of the adult population in Sweden had internet access as compared to only 16% in Portugal; the comparable figures for online shopping being 34% and 1.5% respectively. The Trans-European road and high-speed rail networks will also facilitate convergence. Pan-European media and access to the same entertainment programs through national media are powerful drivers towards cultural conformity. Over the last ten years, pan-European television channels such as MTV or Eurosport have strengthened, and satellite/cable/digital penetration has increased dramatically, albeit with significant country variations–France has increased from 4% to 48% over the period, as compared to 13% to 76% in the UK and from 4% to 22% in Italy (NTC, 2003). Evidence from actual viewing figures suggests that national channels are still the preferred medium, despite these newer media. The print media remain even more nationally based for obvious linguistic and cultural reasons, however there are "niche" media available, such as the Financial Times and the Economist, and national versions of European media, such as Elle, Hello, Burda.

Overriding these trends, a healthy debate continues as to whether, notably in the youth market, the prevailing culture is "Western" or explicitly American due to the prevalence of the US film industry, to US media such as CNN, and especially to the Internet. Also, tourism and migration are extending beyond Europe.

THE IMPACT OF EUROPEAN CONVERGENCE UPON MARKETING DECISIONS

In this section, we build upon the previous analysis of convergence factors and we propose a possible "Euromarketing" convergence framework, taking the key issue of customer convergence as its logical starting point (see Figure 3). We then outline some of the implications of this framework for European marketing decisions.

European drivers may lead to converging European customer traits on the demand side and to a standardized European marketing policy on the supply side. Standardized marketing may have additional conformity influences on customer demand, supported by cost/price effects,

FIGURE 3. European Convergence Framework

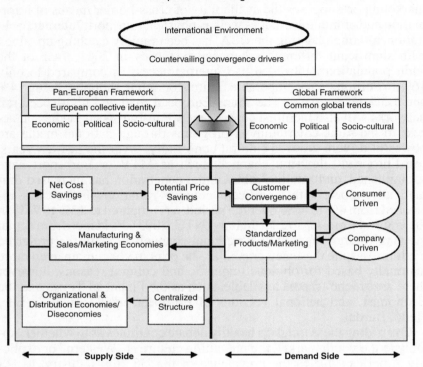

resulting in what amounts to a reinforcing "Euromarketing" convergence framework (Halliburton and Hünerberg, 1993a).

Overall, there is evidence that standardized marketing approaches in Europe have increased in the last decade, post 1993. The early work of Sorenson and Wiechmann (1975) already distinguished between standardization of different elements of the marketing mix amongst European multinationals. More recent work suggests that this has increased– for example, Richter (2002), in a study of major German companies, found that almost the entire marketing mix was standardized to a high degree. Other studies, including those outside of Europe (Chhabra, 1996, Shoham, 1996, Akaah, 1991), have also confirmed the ranked order of such standardization being respectively, product, pricing, promotion, distribution and sales decisions–pricing decisions now being ranked higher than pre-1993.

Firstly we consider the supply side:

- In order to exploit the benefits of pan-European scale, it is beneficial to design identical offers, or quasi-identical offers on the basis of modular systems, for larger target groups. Product elements are standardized the highest extent within the marketing mix (Bolz, 1992; Ozsomer et al., 1991; Shoham, 1996; Richter, 2002). EU standards and legal requirements in many areas support an increasingly Europe-wide policy and EU-specific offerings. Invitations to tender from public authorities force companies into EU wide competition with comparable B-to-B product and service features. Increased mobility, education and exposure to European media and distribution channels also facilitate the introduction of standardized consumer products within the EU. Moreover, financial support in special fields, the ease of intra-EU co-operation and merger and acquisition activities in many cases reinforce the emergence of "Euroconsumer" segments.

There is a positive net effect of European drivers supporting European product and brand strategies, especially standardized offerings; this trend has increased in importance in the last ten years.

- Pricing and financing are increasingly subject to European integration efforts. The most obvious aspect is the common currency in 12 countries, which facilitates customers' price comparisons and pushes companies towards a similar pricing policy. The narrowing of European price corridors has been facilitated by the availability of corresponding media, such as the Internet, by institutions testing goods and by European arbitrage dealers, such as automobile dealers in different EU countries. In addition, financial institutions with European networks and a similar legal framework for pricing and financing (for example, for e-commerce) all support a European price policy. Even outside the present "Eurozone," currency fluctuations are limited and lead to a more stable monetary background for companies' pricing policy. An index of EUROSTAT shows increasing price convergence between EU member states for final consumption (Eurostat, 2003).

Within the EU there are now fewer obstacles to European cross-border pricing; there is a declining opportunity for country-specific pricing approaches in most product markets.

- As outlined earlier, European communication strategies are supported by the existence of European media and/or comparable media in most countries. The legal background within the EU is becoming increasingly harmonized (Krimphove, 2002). Communication agencies are represented in most countries or belong to European networks. Standardized communication leads to cost savings and may help to establish a coherent Europe-wide image, which is of importance for mobile target groups. The advantages of country-specific communication strategies seem to be diminishing, however meanings and associations of verbal and visual signals are culture-bound and therefore frequently require adapted execution around a common communication core concept (Müller, 1996; Whitelock and Pimblett, 1997), including in the former Eastern Europe (Schuh, 2000).

  There is a positive net effect of European drivers supporting European communication campaigns, which has increased in importance in the last ten years; given persistent cultural differences, local execution adaptation may still be required around a common communication core concept.

- In the last ten years cross-border European distribution and retailing have increased. Large retailing companies are present in many European countries, for example, Metro in twenty countries, and Carrefour and Ahold in twelve (IGD (NTC), 2002). There is a common trend towards increased concentration, larger outlets and discounting principles (Euromonitor, 2002). However, significant differences still exist between countries with a greater concentration in northern Europe. For example, over three times as much grocery retail turnover is sold through large supermarket chains in the UK as compared to Italy, which still has over seventy five thousand independent grocers compared to fifteen thousand in the UK (Source: A C Nielsen, 2001). E-commerce is now widely available and, in some fields, well accepted. Internet penetration and shopping habits still show wide differences across Europe, broadly reflecting economic parameters in the wealthier North– 34% on-line shopping habits in Sweden versus under 2% in Portugal (Source: ProActive International, 2001). Retail on-line sites are developing, with Tesco.com, initially in the UK, an early entrant. European logistical services are widely available and rather low-priced due to infrastructure, low distances, competition and recent mergers such as between DHL and Danzas. The legal framework guarantees similar conditions for distribution activities.

There has been a trend towards Pan-European distribution in the last ten years; the underlying drivers suggest that this trend will continue at an increasing rate.

• Whereas ten years ago market information was a barrier to a pan-European approach, many organizations now have databases on a Europe-wide basis and many market research companies have established European networks. Increasing attention is being given to international market research (Craig and Douglas, 2001), with companies such as GFK with its Eurostyles database and Euro-milieus (SINUS). Planning and controlling activities of many companies have now adopted a European centralized or matrix structure. Against this, evidence seems to suggest that companies' internal marketing structures are rather less standardized possibly due to cultural differences, friction between headquarters and country structures and 'not invented here' attitudes (Bolz, 1992; Huszagh et al., 1986; Mazur, 2001; Richter, 2002).

Europe-wide market data is now much more widely available compared to ten years ago and more common planning and controlling techniques are available. However, significant barriers to centralized organization structures appear to persist.

If we now consider the demand side, the evidence seems less conclusive. Whereas legislation, infrastructure and market structure are clear supply-side advantages readily perceived by suppliers, European drivers exercise a less direct influence upon the consumer. This may be due to a lack of awareness of advantages and disadvantages, to conscious and unconscious resistance to change, and to deep-rooted national or regional preferences, which may literally be centuries old in some markets:

• Studies of Euroconsumer convergence over the last ten years show contrasting results. Country, or even local, preferences persist in many markets, implying the need for cross-border differentiation. For example, food products still show persistent national traditions and even the major multinationals have had to preserve local brands alongside their pan-European products, such as Unilever with Miko ice-cream in France, Wall's in the UK and Agnesi in Italy, or Danone with Lu biscuits in Western Europe and Opavia in eastern Europe. Some authors have integrated cross-cultural management research to support this analysis (Steenkamp, 2001). However, there is some evidence that the increasing pan-European approaches of companies together with the advances in European integration have contributed to increasing similarity of buying habits and demand. A number of authors have identified European country clusters of similar behavior characteristics (Askegaard and Madsen, 1998; Michalski and Tallberg, 1999). To summarize:

Despite the persistence of entrenched national or local preferences in more context-specific markets, there has been a positive trend towards increasing 'pan-European' consumer behavior in many product markets.

STRATEGIC OPTIONS
FOR A EUROPEAN MARKETING APPROACH

Figure 4 summarizes some of the strategic options resulting from the six propositions outlined above, relating these to different segmentation approaches and consequent product offerings.

Companies face three interdependent factors when formulating their strategic marketing options–*geographic, target groups* and *product/service offerings* (Hünerberg, 1994, p. 97).

The first concerns the *geographic area* to be covered. There are many possibilities ranging from a global to a local approach. Pan-European market selection belongs to a sub-global strategy and if not the whole of Europe, but only parts are selected, then this can be categorized as a sub-European approach. A sub-global strategy beyond Europe is also possible, for example the combination of the US and UK markets. The areas selected within a Europe-oriented strategy may consist of several countries and/or areas defined across traditional country borders, for example, a segment may comprise parts of Germany and France. These areas may be physically contiguous within Europe or not, such as the population of major European capitals, or Gillette's pan-Atlantic product strategy.

Secondly, the *target groups* must be defined, as distinct from the geographic segmentation, with traditional segmentation criteria applied.

FIGURE 4. Strategic European Marketing Options

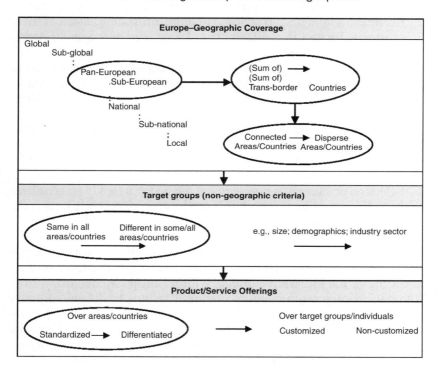

Thirdly, *product/service* offerings have to be tailored to the selected target groups in the defined geographic areas. The crucial question is to which degree they can be standardized geographically as well as customized to different target groups or even to individuals within the target groups. It should be borne in mind that this decision can vary over the different marketing instruments–for example, a standardized product offering across all target groups in all countries may be advertised in a rather differentiated way.

The combination of these three factors leads to a number of possible strategic European marketing options–(options 1 to 4 could also be combined with segments outside Europe):

1. European segments consisting of a selection of countries–all of these segments treated in a differentiated way. For example, the

beer market exhibits marked country differences, with distinct brands and differentiated advertising and packaging approaches.

2. European segments, all or some of them, cross-border–all of these segments treated in a differentiated way. For example, "Euroregions" or the major financial centers.

3. European segments consisting of a selection of countries–all or some of them treated in a standardized way. For example, Northern, Central and "Southern/Mediterranean" Europe with differences in climate and seasonality effects.

4. European segments, all or some of them, cross-border–all or some of these segments treated in a standardized way. For example, the youth market in major capitals with products such as Caterpillar footwear/apparel.

5. Selection of Europe as one segment, treated in a totally standardized way. For example, certain b-2-b services, or automobile brands designed for the pan-European market.

Whereas option 5 constitutes a totally pan-European approach, option 1 is the contrary, distinct national segments. Option 2 takes into account some of the integrative effects within Europe by departing from traditional country segmentation. Option 3 retains traditional country segmentation but assumes similarities over countries. Option 4 combines cases 2 and 3. If the previously outlined convergence effects are valid, and increase in the future, then options 2 to 4 will increase in importance, and possibly also the "pure" pan-European option 5.

CONCLUSIONS AND FURTHER MANAGEMENT IMPLICATIONS

In this article the authors argue that in the last ten years the drivers towards European conformity override the tendencies towards divergence. This is especially true for the supply-side factors where the effects of EU integration efforts result in many specific and uniform market conditions. They indirectly also support demand-side convergence. If these premises are valid, then companies' market selection decisions will increasingly involve strategic options, which imply some form of Euro-segmentation. In a very long-term perspective, this may be a transitory phase towards a fully global approach.

The article also proposes a European convergence framework intended as a possible basis for further empirical research, investigating the operational implications as to how the EU-integration process will continue to impact upon specific marketing activities.

Increasingly, cross-border European markets are a reality and companies with European marketing approaches with more or less standardized strategies, operations and processes already exist. Over the ten-year period since the symbolic SEM date of 1993 pan-European marketing indeed appears to be more of an "emerging reality." Companies therefore must find ways to reconcile simultaneously the advantages of pan-European scale with increasing customer demand for choice and persistent differences in national or regional consumer preferences–what we have called elsewhere "global individualism." They will therefore need to be much better informed as to social and technology trends within Europe, to the new media and emerging distribution channels. They must develop new ways to handle transnational customer relationships and to exploit the benefits of European one-to-one marketing. They will need to adopt new organizational solutions, management styles and new sources of information in Europe. They will need to:

- Establish which countries or parts of countries are inherently interesting, on the basis of fundamental considerations such as population, income, demand, and infrastructure.
- Discover whether cross-border segments are sufficiently significant, with similar demand criteria.
- Establish suitable market accessibility, as well as harmonized supply-side conditions.
- Finally, decide which marketing instruments can be standardized over which segments and to which extent, again taking into account demand and supply-side market conditions.

As a concluding example, Hildebrand and Simon (2000) considered the European market for bathroom equipment. Their conclusions were: negligible trade barriers, low transport costs, increasing price convergence towards lower prices, similar distribution channels in most countries, increasing cross-border retailing, converging consumer tastes, and international designer products matching Europe-wide product standards. Generally, pan-European competition is now the rule in this market.

As a final comment, future research is needed to formulate more specific hypotheses based upon the premises outlined above and to test these across countries and industry sectors/product categories as we would caution against overgeneralizations across product areas. Such research could take the form of empirical investigation of the European marketing practices of EU-based and non-EU companies, of longitudinal studies and expert panels to assess relevant developments, and questionnaire-based research on different marketing instruments.

REFERENCES

Akaah, P.I. (1991). Strategy Standardisation in International Marketing: An Empirical Investigation of Its Degree of Use and Correlates. *Journal of Global Marketing*, 4(2), 39-62.

Altmann, F-L. (2001). Formation of National Identities; Regional and Transnational Identities. In: *Proceedings of the Colloquy of the Council of Europe "The Concept of Identity,"* Strasbourg, 17th/18th April.

Askegaard, S., & Madsen, T.K. (1998). The Local and the Global: Exploring Traits of Homogeneity and Heterogeneity in European Food Cultures. *International Business Review*, 7(6), 549-568.

Bolz, J. (1992). *Wettbewerbsorientierte Standardisierung der Internationalen Marktbearbeitung: Eine Empirische Anaylse der Europäischen Sclüsselmärkte*. Universitäts Verlag, Darmstadt.

Chhabra, S.S. (1996). Marketing Adaptation by Multinational Corporations in South America. *Journal of Global Marketing*, 9(4), 57-74.

Commission Regulation (EC) No. 1400/2002 (2002). Commission Regulation (EC) No. 1400/2002 of 31 July 2002 on the Application of Article 81 (3) of the Treaty to Categories of Vertical Agreements and Concerted Practices in the Motor Vehicle Sector. In *Official Journal of the European Communities*, L 203/30, 1st August, 2002.

Craig, C.S. & Douglas, S. (2001). Conducting International Marketing Research in the Twenty-first Century. *International Marketing Review*, 18(1), 80-90.

Emmanouilidis, J.A., & Giering, C. (2003). *Light and Shade–An Evaluation of the Convention's Proposals*, from *http://www.cap.uni-muenchen.de/konvent/spotlight/Spotlight_08-03_e.pdf*

Euromonitor Plc., (Ed.), (2002). *European Marketing Data and Statistics 2002*, 37th edition, London.

Eurostat (2002). *Jahrbuch* 2002. Luxembourg.

Eurostat (2003). *Price Convergence between EU Member States–Coefficient of Variation of Comparative Price Levels of Final Consumption by Private Households Including Indirect Taxes,* from *http://europa.eu.int/comm/eurostat/Public/datashop/print-product/EN?catalogue=Eurostat&product=1-er012-EN&mode=download*

Ghemawat, P. (2003). Semiglobalization and International Business Strategy. *Journal of International Business Studies*, 34(2), 138-152.

Grein, A. (2000). The Impact of Market Similarity on International Marketing Strategies: The Automobile Industry in Western Europe. *Thunderbird International Business Review*, 42(2), 167-179.

Haller, M. (1999). Voiceless Submission or Deliberate Choice? European Integration and the Relation Between National and European Identity. In Kriese et al., (Eds.),

Nation and National Identity. The European Experience in Perspective, Chur–Zürich, 261-296.

Halliburton, C., & Hünerberg, R. (1993). Pan-European Marketing–Myth or Reality? *Journal of International Marketing*, 1(3), 77-92.

Halliburton, C., & Hünerberg, R. (1993). *European Marketing; Readings and Cases*, Reading 1.1, London, Addison-Wesley.

Hildebrand, D., & Simon, H. (2000). Basisoptionen Internationaler Wettbewerbsstrategien. In Zentes et al. (Ed), *Fallstudien zum Internationalen Management*, Wiesbaden.

Hofstede, F.T., Steenkamp, J-B.E.M. & Wedel, M. (1999). International Market Segmentation Based on Consumer-Product Relations. *Journal of Marketing Research*, 36(1), 1-17.

Hofstede, F.T., Wedel, M. & Steenkamp, J-B.E.M. (2002). Identifying Spatial Segments in International Markets. *Marketing Science*, 21(2), 160-177.

Hünerberg, R. (1994). *Internationales Marketing*, Landsberg.

Huszagh, S., Fox, R.J. & Day, E. (1985). Global Marketing: An Empirical Investigation. *Columbia Journal of World Business*, 21, 31-44.

Jallat, F. & Kimmel, A.J. (2002). Marketing in Culturally Diverse Environments: The Case of Western Europe. *Business Horizons*, 45(4), 30-36.

Jansen, T., (Ed.), (1999), *Reflections on European Identity*. Working Paper (Forward Studies Unit of the European Commission), Brussels.

Karklins, R. (2001). The Concept of Collective Identity. In *Proceedings of the Colloquy of the Council of Europe "The Concept of Identity,"* Strasbourg, 17th/18th April.

Kotler, P. (1984). The Ad.Biz Goes Global. *Fortune*, 12 November, 61-64.

Krimphove, D. (2002). *Europäisches Werberecht*, München.

Leeflang, P.S.H., & van Raaij, W.F. (1995). The changing consumer in the European Union: A 'Meta-analysis.' *International Journal of Research in Marketing*,12(5), 373-387.

Levitt, T. (1983). The Globalization of Markets. *Harvard Business Review*, 61(3), 92-102.

Lewis, C. & Vickerstaff, A. (2001). Beer Branding in British and Czech Companies: A Comparative Study. *Marketing Intelligence & Planning*, 19(5), 341-350.

Mazur, L. (2001). Brands Return to a Pan-European Marketing Style. *Marketing*, 6/14/2001, 1-3.

Michalski, A., & Tallberg, J. (1999). *Project on European Integration Indicators. People's Europe*. Working Paper, (Forward Studies Unit of the European Commission), Brussels.

Müller, W.G. (1996). Die Standardisierbarkeit Internationaler Werbung: Kulturen Verlangen Adaptionen. *Marketing ZFP*, 3, 179-190.

NTC Publications (Ed.), (2002). *The Marketing Pocket Book 2003*, Henley-on-Thames.

NTC Publications (Ed.), (1993). *The Marketing Pocket Book 1994*, Henley-on-Thames.

Ozsomer, A., Bodur, M., & Cavusgil, S.T. (1991). Marketing Standardisation by Multinationals in an Emerging Market. *European Journal of Marketing*, 25(12), 50-64.

Pasco, M. (2001). Euro-youth: Myth or Reality? *Admap*, 36(6), 14-15.

Richter, T. (2001). *Marketing Mix Standardization in International Marketing*, Peter Lang, Frankfurt.

Savitt, R. (1998). This Thing I Call Europe. *International Marketing Review*, 15(6), 444-446.

Schuh, A. (2000). Global Standardization as a Success Formula for Marketing in Central Eastern Europe. *Journal of World Business*, 35(2), 133-148.

Shoham, A. (1996). Marketing-mix Standardization. *Journal of Global Marketing*, 10 (2), 91-119.

Sorenson, R.Z., & Wiechmann, U.E. (1975). How Multinationals View Marketing Standardization. *Harvard Business Review*, May-June, 38-54.

Steenkamp, J-B.E.M. (2001). The Role of National Culture in International Marketing Research. *International Marketing Review*, 18(1), 30-44.

Voigt, S., & Schmidt, A. (2003). *Making European Merger Policy More Predictable.* (European Round Table of Industrialists) Brussels.

Whitelock, J.M. & Pimblett, C. (1997). The Standardization Debate in International Marketing. *Journal of Global Marketing*, 10(3), 45-66.

Marketing Consequences of European Internal Market Unification: An Executive Perspective

Don Sciglimpaglia
Massoud Saghafi

SUMMARY. The European Union (EU) is now ten years old and many of the hundreds of directives envisioned by its founding members are now in place. From an international marketing perspective, what has the EU's internal market really achieved over the past decade? This study may be the first of its kind to address the marketing implications of the European single market formation from the perspective of the European corporate managers. In particular, the study addresses progress in the harmonization of marketing programs, effectiveness and efficiency of post-unification marketing in the EU and resulting effects on marketing strategy in the EU over ten years. While the results of this study point to significant progress towards a more pan-European marketing strategy, the European executives who participated in our study suggest that results are not uniform over all areas of the marketing function. *[Article copies available for a fee from The Haworth Document Delivery Service: 1-800-HAWORTH. E-mail address: <docdelivery@haworthpress.com> Website: <http://www.HaworthPress. com>* © 2004 by The Haworth Press, Inc. All rights reserved.]*

Don Sciglimpaglia is Professor of Marketing and Massoud Saghafi is Professor of Marketing, both at San Diego State University.

Address correspondence to: Don Sciglimpaglia, Department of Marketing, San Diego State University, San Diego, CA 92182 (E-mail: dsciglim@mail.sdsu.edu).

[Haworth co-indexing entry note]: "Marketing Consequences of European Internal Market Unification: An Executive Perspective." Sciglimpaglia, Don and Massoud Saghafi. Co-published simultaneously in *Journal of Euromarketing* (International Business Press, an imprint of The Haworth Press, Inc.) Vol. 14, No. 1/2, 2004, pp. 35-57; and: *Marketing Issues in Western Europe: Changes and Developments* (eds: Erdener Kaynak, and Frédéric Jallat) International Business Press, an imprint of The Haworth Press, Inc., 2004, pp. 35-57. Single or multiple copies of this article are available for a fee from The Haworth Document Delivery Service [1-800-HAWORTH, 9:00 a.m. - 5:00 p.m. (EST). E-mail address: docdelivery@haworthpress.com].

KEYWORDS. Europe, internal market unification, EU expansion/enlargement, European Monetary Unit, marketing mix standardization, pan-European marketing strategy, single market

INTRODUCTION

Even though academics, practitioners and policy makers across the world are now cheering the successful integration of the EU, their views were not always positive (Boddewyn and Grosse, 1995). In fact, American skeptics viewed the creation of the EU, its eastward expansion plan and the launching of the euro as mere political rather than economic moves: ". . . there has always been something surreptitious about the movement for European unity, a political objective shrouded in economic language . . ." (Will, 1997). Such beliefs still linger on, even after the successful launch of the euro: ". . . changes like the euro and EU enlargement are seldom justified on economic grounds . . . they are really political moon shots cleverly marketed as economic breakthroughs . . ." (Dowling, 2002).

From a European perspective, another explanation for the formation and expansion of EU may be the fact that given the enormous economic power of the United States and its sheer market size, a unified European market could be more competitive than and as attractive as the American market. The Lisbon Summit of 2002 confirmed this belief when it set the ambitious goal of turning the EU into the world's most dynamic and competitive knowledge-based economy by 2010 (Norman, 2002). Furthermore, a unified EU economy could withstand trade disputes with the United States, Japan and other international commercial powers. For example, the EU was the first of WTO members to file a formal complaint against US steel tariffs (for which it received a favorable ruling in July 2003) and the French, backed by the entire EU, have successfully challenged Microsoft's pricing strategy, claiming that the company's French versions sold in France are priced higher than French versions sold in Canada (*Wall Street Journal*, April 6, 2000).

The introduction of the euro has also turned out to be a major success. It has reduced exchange rate risks and transaction costs in member states and stimulated European mergers, acquisitions and cross-border deals. Lewis (2000), in an evaluative study, reported that intra-European Monetary Unit (EMU) area trade grew by 8% between August 1998 and August 1999, while external exports rose by just 3% over the same period. As an example, the European chemicals industry has experienced savings resulting largely from the reduction in the number of foreign exchange transactions (Blanco, 2001). These efficiency gains are expected to spill over into other EU industry sectors.

What do all of these developments mean for marketers? Theories aside, there is little empirical evidence on the overall impact of the single market formation on the marketing strategy of global companies. Has the marketing function become more Pan-European, or do marketers still view the EU as a set of individual entities requiring different marketing strategies? Is there any marketing-mix variable (price, promotion and advertising, distribution and product) that has become more Pan-European? The purpose of this study is to provide answers to the above questions from the perspective of EU managers.

EU FORMATION AND MARKETING MIX STANDARDIZATION

International marketing theory suggests that the necessary condition for a successful standardized marketing strategy is uniformity of the marketing environment. This includes harmonization of legal-regulatory issues, economics, cultural and technical conditions in the selected region and for the selected target segment. Of course, no two countries present identical environments, nor is that required. What is necessary, however, is uniformity in the environmental conditions that influence marketing variables. Has there been a marked environmental convergence across the European Union since 1993?

Although the legal environment remained a major obstacle for a Euro-marketing strategy in the early stages of the single market formation (Hildebrand, 1994), many marketing-related legal issues are moving towards harmonization. Indeed, the European Union has developed both an advanced regional set of competitive rules and a model of supranational governance in which regulatory decisions on competition rest with a 20-member EU Commission (McGowan, 1998). At the macroeconomics level, there are still differences in income levels, employment statistics, consumer expenditures and patterns of consumption between the EU countries, as reported by Wierenga, Pruyn and Waarts (1996). On the consumer-side, a homogenization of cultural values, consumer wants and preferences may be underway, but that is a dialectic process. There are still differences in the EU with respect to family structures and decision processes. There are also considerable differences in education, language and religious values (Wierenga, Pruyn and Waarts, 1996).

In short, although, in theory, environmental convergence was expected across the EU, in practice, complete environmental harmonization may be a long way away. The legal policy environment appears to have shown the greatest advances towards harmonization, while the cultural environment has lagged behind. Given the debate on the environmental convergence and the trends in marketing-mix variables, the question of a pan-European vs. a country-by-country marketing strategy is still an open debate, even though attempts have been made to suggest the supremacy of one or the other (Diamantopoulos, Schlegelmilch and Du Preez, 1995). The economic rationale behind the formation of the single European market has always been efficiency in production and distribution as well as effectiveness in customer satisfaction. Pre-1993, speculation on marketing variables concentrated on harmonization. Indeed, US firms were advised to develop strategic alliances with European companies, standardize product lines, reduce costs, and be aware of and adapt to legal changes in the EU in order to remain competitive in a unified Europe (Reilly, 1995).

Product Issues

Product standardization has been the most hotly debated international marketing topic among academics, as well as practitioners, for decades. However, practice has shown that, though standardization worked for product categories such as consumer electronics, not every product travels well, even across a relatively homogeneous economic market. There are some very simple rules, which have to be observed if a product is to be accepted across a number of markets. Pan-European marketing certainly makes sense from a distribution and economic point of view, but marketers should understand that the "new" Europe is still a series of regional, if not national, markets displaying strong local characteristics. Similarly, the paradox of market globalization combined with intra-national fragmentation of consumer needs prompts Hofstede, Wedel and Steenkamp (2002) to suggest cross-national consumer segmentation based on needs and identification of spatial consumer segments using survey data collected among consumers in seven EU countries.

Pricing Issues

The research on price harmonization across the EU is equivocal. The debate focuses not only on whether uniform EU pricing is possible but on the basic issue of its economic logic (Blanco, 2001). Verdin and van Heck (2000) posit that the assumption of price homogenization for consumer goods grossly underestimates the existence of differences across Europe beyond currency differentials. They suggest that market integration need not eliminate price discrimination or segmentation (as it has not in the United States). On the contrary, it may provide opportunities for more segmentation rather than less–but on economic criteria rather than artificial geographic ones. On the other hand, the formation of large retailers with global purchasing and distribution strategy, the proliferation of parallel imports and the introduction of the euro may force some degree of price harmonization across the European Union.

Distribution Issues

The move to an EU-wide distribution orientation has not been consistent across industries. While the chemicals industry has achieved this goal and the automotive industry is well on its way, other industries, such as pharmaceuticals and electronics, have been slowed in their progress by the large number of local restrictions (Poist, Scheraga and Semeijn, 2001). Even those companies looking to develop a Europe-wide logistics services orientation have found themselves looking to third-party carriers (Anderson and Katz, 1998). Furthermore, noticeable differences in distribution systems, especially at the retailing level, are also present across the EU that inhibit a standard approach to EU-wide distribution (Wierenga, Pruyn and Waarts, 1996).

The logistics function was believed to significantly benefit from an EU-wide strategic orientation with the anticipation of more efficient transportation networks. This is primarily the result of reducing unnecessary costs associated with existing fragmentation, duplication, and border delays. However, both such *external* obstacles as transport infrastructure and the resistance of customers to changing their distribution strategies and *internal* inhibiting forces as quality of management, culture and local politics have presented a demanding challenge to the logistics manager who has to confront an uneven implementation of the EU framework (Priemus et al., 1998; Skjoett-Larsen, 1998; Pelkmans, 1992).

The existence of pan-European or regional channels of distribution points some manufacturers towards a more standard marketing approach. Food retailers, for example, are developing business at a pan-European level, often through the formation of pan-European mergers and alliances (Jakubowski, 1995). Nevertheless, despite the ongoing economic unification in the EU, it is still too early to talk about a unified set of European *marketing* theories and practices. Harmonization appears to be a possible objective at the pan-European level as a medium to long-term objective, although difficult in the short run (McGowan, 1998; Jallat and Kimmel, 2002).

Advertising and Promotion Issues

As the process of emerging into a single market continues, marketers and, particularly, advertisers of multinational products must concern themselves with presenting a unified brand image. However, given the importance of culture on the four basic advertising elements mentioned above, MNCs must not only focus on the benefits of economies of scale when advertising, but also on the needs of and differences in their target markets. The emergence of a single European market may not mean a market that is culturally homogeneous, thus may make "Euro-ads," an expensive strategy with failing results (Seitz, 1998). Indeed differences and incoherent strategies still exist in the advertising and media environment in EU (Berns-Wright and Morgan, 2002). Standardized marketing approach for the whole EU is still a far away perspective for most manufacturers.

Pan-European Marketing Strategy Issues

The standardization of marketing strategy has been debated for decades in academia, and many researchers have addressed this issue (Levitt, 1983; Jain 1989; Baalbaki and Malhotra, 1995; Whitelock and Pimblett, 1997). However, long before the peak of the academic discussion on standardization of marketing programs, the British adverting agency Saatchi and Saatchi had already developed a global advertising campaign for British Airways.

Saghafi, Sciglimpaglia and Withers (1995) conducted a major study early in the market unification process to predict the eventual outcomes of the EC 92 directives. A survey instrument was mailed to the executives of international companies to solicit their expectations on the general business environment and specific marketing conditions in the post-unification EU. The results of the survey provided a first round insight into the expected marketing implications of the international EU market formation for the manufacturing sector.

In general, the expectation of the executives surveyed was favored further environmental convergence, product standardization and a more harmonized pan-European marketing strategy over the long run. It was also predicted that pan-European branding and packaging, common product introduction and positioning, and EU-wide segmentation strategies were expected to replace a country-by-country product strategy. Pan European advertising was expected to be strongly favored by industrial marketers in the post-1993 EU, even though advertising and promotional cost savings were in doubt due to higher competitive pressures and the perceived intensity of such activities.

There was also a strong expectation among the EU marketers that the prices of manufactured goods would equalize across Europe and that demand and competitive differences would be dealt with via the use of "special deals" to distributors (Saghafi, Sciglimpaglia and Withers, 1995). Research conducted by the European Commission confirmed that price disparities in Europe declined between 1985 and 1993 due to increasing competition and globalization of the EU economy but the decline in price disparity slowed between 1993 and 1996 (Blanco, 2001).

A single market also provides opportunities for reducing inventories as well as warehousing sites, and permits greater consolidation of transport loads and development of more efficient route structures. Likewise, a borderless market allows for faster and more reliable services from a central or limited number of stock locations (Poist, Scheraga and Semeijn, 2001). Channel consolidation and cross-border cooperation among distributors were also expected to rise in the post-1993 Europe, all leading to further distribution efficiency (Saghafi, Sciglimpaglia and Withers, 1995). Indeed, some companies had already reported that their total logistics costs have been reduced by as much as 40-50 percent (O'Laughlin et al., 1993).

Leeflang and van Raaij (1995), studying the changing EU consumers, find that although large cross-sectional differences still exist, some common trends are clearly present. They conclude that the EU nations are converging towards a more similar macro-marketing environment and require a more similar macro-marketing mix. They then declare ". . . Euromarketing is the name of the game for the future." Kouremenos and Avlonitis (1995) support the above findings and suggest that since joining the EU in the 1980s, Greek consumers moved much closer to their "average" European counterparts in terms of consumption patterns, life styles, social attitudes and demographics. Further support for the "convergence" theory of EU customers is provided by Ganesh (1998) who suggests that increased convergence mandates that firms must rethink their strategies for operating in the EU. Regarding European countries as very different market entities that require different marketing strategies may no longer be an efficient way to conduct business in the EU. Conversely, this convergence does not imply treating 400 million consumers as one homogeneous unit served by a single set of standardized product, promotion, and distribution strategies. Culture and other environmental variations still exist across the EU. Convergence findings however suggest a "blending of lifestyles and growing uniformity in consumer tastes and purchasing behavior that will progressively minimize traditional geographical and political boundaries" (Ganesh, 1998).

While the general expectations on EU-wide marketing is towards stronger integration of the marketing strategy, there are still those academicians who believe the environmental differences will not allow successful Pan-European marketing practice in the short or medium run. Kale (1995) argues that the move toward European integration should entail major adjustments in a firm's marketing strategy ". . . despite the dismantling of legislative barriers, cultural milieu of the various member nations will continue to be an obstacle toward true integration." He further develops three distinct cultural clusters among European countries, each with its unique cultural composition and alludes to the necessity of three distinct cultural-based marketing strategies for each cluster. Steenkamp and Hofstede (1999), using a large sample of consumers from eleven EU countries, measured differences in consumer innovativeness across the EU. They concluded that indeed, significant differences between the level of innovation among members is directly affected by differences in individual disposition. These are, in turn, affected by overall national cultural differences that are different across the EU. Wierenga, Pruyn and Waarts (1996) studying the consumer behavior across the EU conclude that ". . . there are tremendous differences in income levels and income spending patterns among the countries of the European Union and also major differences with respect to consumer values and lifestyles. Furthermore, the distribution and retailing environments as well as the media, differ considerably from one country to another." A completely standardized marketing strategy for the EU is still unrealistic. Furthermore ". . . despite broad cultural similarities, the EU is not yet a single market for advertisers. Nor can the same advertisement be run in both the United States and the EU. Businesses and consumers both would benefit from a consistent regulation of advertising. Over the long term, further harmonization appears inevitable" (Petty, 1997).

In short, several developments have clearly occurred that *theoretically* should lead to convergence and homogenization of marketing practice.

1. The EU directives and subsequent decisions have indubitably paved the way for structural harmonization of the business environment.
2. The ISO and similar standards are now adopted Europe-wide and indeed globally.
3. The industrial regulatory and policymaking environments from pharmaceuticals to telecommunications have become unified (Steinert, 1998).
4. The ethical-legal environment governing corporate conduct and punishments for organizational misconduct have harmonized within the EU (Thorne-LeClair, Farrell and Farrell, 1997; Thorne-LeClair, 2000).
5. From the economic environment perspective, the competitive pressures set loose by the euro's introduction have ensured moderate wage and price rises: ". . . the euro is already cementing in place many of the conditions required for stable prices and long-term growth" (Barber, 2002).

It appears that the harmonization of the economic, political, legal, regulatory, and technology environments in the EU have somewhat advanced and, eventually, may lead to a unified marketing infrastructure across the EU. However, cultural convergence has lagged behind. Academic research is still equivocal on the degree of homogenization of EU markets and the extent to which marketers can standardize price, promotion, distribution and their product/service offering. Indeed, ten years after the formation of the European single market, we are still largely uncertain as to its impact from an international marketing perspective. This present study is perhaps the first of its kind to evaluate the marketing developments of the past ten years in the European Union from the perspective of the marketing practitioners. We investigate the direction of marketing strategy in the EU over the past ten years and consider future trends in the European Union.

PURPOSE OF THE STUDY

The primary objective of this study is to investigate the impacts of Europe's internal market creation and evolution over the past decade on strategic marketing decisions as practiced by EU companies. Our specific interest is to delineate any marked movement towards a pan-European marketing strategy as undertaken by EU companies over the period of 1993-2003. To do this, we set out to survey top executives from a cross-section of industries in the EU to ascertain their opinions on the changes in strategy they had witnessed over the prior ten years.

Specifically, this study addresses the following issues:

1. Has the creation of the European internal market led to harmonization of the marketing strategy and to pan-European marketing?
2. Have the cost efficiencies in marketing that were expected to follow as a result of more efficient distribution and logistics, pan-European advertising and promotion and standard product design and manufacturing materialized?
3. Have European companies become more efficient globally due to the scale economies, harmonized trade environments and economic consolidations?

Methodology

Many of the questions and items in the research were derived from prior studies, notably the research of Saghafi, Sciglimpaglia and Withers (1995), which attempted early on to assess the likelihood of occurrence of the effects of the internal market on business operations and markets. In addition, an e-mail survey was conducted among leading scholars to request input on important or timely issues. To conduct the survey, an attempt was made to locate online sources which could provide an e-mail sample of European business executives. Using the services of 24/7 Media Inc., a leading Internet marketing services provider, the opt-in e-mail list of economist.com was selected. Economist.com is the online site of Economist magazine, a widely respected resource for business news in Europe. The opt-in resource represents a permission e-mail file with searchable respondent characteristics. Using this capability, a sample was developed limited to the following database characteristics:

Location of firm:	France, Germany, Netherlands and UK
Number of employees of firm:	500-999, 1,000-4,999, 5,000-9,999 and 10,000 or more

Responsibility:	Corporate planning, general management, international operations, manufacturing/production and sales/marketing
Title:	Board Director, CEO, Chairman, COO, Department Head, Executive, General Manager, Managing Director, Owner/Partner, President, Vice President and Middle Manager

In all, a total sample of 5,000 e-mail addresses was selected from a wide range of industries.

An e-mail message was sent to each potential respondent by economist.com requesting participation in an important academic study of the effects of the EU internal market. At the bottom of the e-mail message was a hyperlink which took the potential respondent to an online survey developed using Perseus Development's Survey Solutions for the Web, a leading online survey package. The survey questionnaire consisted of a number of statements regarding the effects of the EU internal market. Respondents were asked to rate their degree of agreement to each, using a seven point, balanced Likert scale, anchored at strongly agree (7) and strongly disagree (1). As an incentive an offer was made to donate 500 euros to a charitable organization selected by respondents. It is not possible to know how many of the 5,000 e-mail addresses were still active at the time of the survey. However, Internet server tracking showed that 1,237 from the sample opened the e-mail message (24.7%). Of these, 188 clicked through to the survey and 87 completed the survey online. The proportion of those who saw the survey that actually responded was quite high, roughly 46%.

RESULTS

Table 1 shows the details on the 87 respondents to the survey. Nearly all are corporate executives located in the EU, with the majority located in the UK or in Germany. Roughly three-quarters represent European companies, with the remainder mainly representing American firms located in Europe. The respondents currently serve as top level executives or directors, department heads, or middle managers. The major areas of responsibility of these executives are sales or marketing management, international operations, and corporate planning. The majority of these

TABLE 1. Characteristics of Survey Respondents

In what country is your company headquarters located?

UK	25	28.7%
Germany	13	14.9
France	11	12.6
Netherlands	10	11.5
Other EU country	4	4.6
US	19	21.8
Other North or South American country	2	2.3
Japan	1	1.1
Other Asian country	<u>2</u>	<u>2.2</u>
	87	100.0%

What is your current company location?

UK	38	43.7%
Germany	14	16.1
France	15	17.2
Netherlands	13	14.9
Other EU country	2	2.3
US	3	3.4
Other North or South American country	1	1.1
Asian country [not Japan]	<u>1</u>	<u>1.1</u>
	87	100.0%

What is your title or position?

CEO	1	1.1
Board Director	6	6.9
Executive	10	11.5
Managing Director	8	9.2
Company President	2	2.3
General Manager	6	6.9
Department Head	16	18.4
Vice President	5	5.7
Middle manager	25	28.7
Other	<u>8</u>	<u>9.1</u>
	87	100.0%

What is your main area of responsibility?

Corporate planning	10	11.5%
General management	16	18.4
International operations	15	17.2
Manufacturing or production	6	6.9
Sales or marketing	19	21.8
Other	<u>21</u>	<u>24.1</u>
	87	100.0%

What is the size of your company?

Under 500 employees	14	16.1%
500-999	4	4.6
1,000-4,999	19	21.8
5,000-9,999	10	11.5
10,000 or more employees	<u>40</u>	<u>46.0</u>
	87	100.0%

Which of the following best describes your industry?

Professional services	5	5.7%
Energy extraction	1	1.1
Management consultancy	5	5.7
Chemical or metal processing	1	1.1
I.T. services	8	9.2
Engineering	2	2.2
Manufacturing	15	17.2
Government	2	2.3
Construction	2	2.3
Distribution	5	5.7
Publishing	8	9.2
Transport & communications	8	9.2
Pharmaceutical	3	3.4
Banking	7	4.6
Financial services/accountancy	4	4.6
Insurance/real estate	4	4.6
Other	<u>14</u>	<u>16.1</u>
	87	100.0%

What are the main end-use markets for your business?

Mainly consumer	30	34.1%
Roughly equally consumer and business/industrial use	16	18.2
Mainly business/industrial	<u>41</u>	<u>47.7</u>
	87	100.0%

respondents represent large firms with 5,000 or more employees. The firms occupy a wide range of industries, with the greatest concentration in the areas of manufacturing, transportation, communications, and IT services. Companies represented span the range of consumer and business markets.

To summarize the results of the survey, responses have been categorized by the percent in agreement with each statement, representing "strongly agree," "agree" and "somewhat agree." Otherwise, the respondent generally disagreed with the statement, or neither agreed nor disagreed.

Product Issues

Executives surveyed clearly feel that the impact of EU market integration on products and services available in Europe has been significant. (See Table 2.) Over seventy percent of our respondents (71.6%) report that overall product quality has increased since the inception of the internal market. Also impressive has been an increase in variety of products made available to businesses and organizations (75.9%) and to consumers (67.1%). As one respondent indicated, ". . . borderless markets have increased product diversification and availability."

Another major impact has been on the production side. Firms are seen as being able to achieve greater scale economies by producing more standardized products (64.3%) which led to this being a fairly common practice (61.4%). This is exemplified by the comments of respondents to the survey, who indicated ". . . ability to centralize manufacturing" and "European norms allow the sale of our products across the EU without further testing and certifications" as being major influences. As might be anticipated, the effects appear greater for products as opposed to services. This is echoed by two respondents who said, ". . . a service company is still mainly bound to local culture and language" and ". . . effect is less strong for a services company," although one indicated ". . . my company is a parcel express company and the single market has simplified operations and marketing."

This, in turn, is related to branding strategies. Most (53.0%) report the Eurobranding has become a common practice. Consequently, new product introduction throughout the EU, rather than on a country-by-country level, is seen as typical strategy for about one half of all respondents (45.9%). Conversely, the majority do not see country specific product positioning disappearing, with only about one-in-three (36.1%) agreeing that this has disappeared. From a management perspective, roughly half of the executives surveyed feel that EU market integration has affected product brand positioning strategy (45.3%) and brand management tactical decisions (44.7%). Given all of these changes, surprisingly, only about one-third (35.4%) of these executives feel that the integration of the EU markets has increased the rate of product innovation in their industry.

Pricing Issues–Price Levels and Competitiveness

The impact of the EU single market on prices and on pricing strategy is most interesting. (See Table 3.) First, against all expectations, only

TABLE 2. Product Planning Issues

Statement	Mean Score	Percent Agree*
Manufacturing of standardized Europroducts has become commonplace.	4.36	61.4
Variety of products available to EU consumers has increased.	4.81	67.1
Variety of products available to EU business and organizations has increased.	4.98	75.9
In general, spending on new product development (percent of sales) has increased for companies located in the EU.	3.92	37.8
Companies have been able to achieve greater economy of scale in production by reducing the need to make changes in products for specific EU countries.	4.58	64.3
New product introduction throughout the entire EU, rather than by country, is now very common.	4.14	45.9
Products positioned by country within the EU are disappearing in favor of EU-wide positioning.	3.70	36.1
The integration of EU markets positively affected your company's brand management for strategic issues (targeting and positioning).	4.20	45.3
The integration of EU markets positively affected your company's brand management for tactical issues (logo, visual and packaging).	3.96	44.7
The integration of EU markets has increased the rate of product innovation in your industry.	3.74	35.4
Compared to ten years ago, overall product quality has increased for EU manufacturers.	4.99	71.6
Eurobranding has become a commonplace practice.	4.36	53.0

*Statement equals Somewhat Agree (5), Agree (6) and Strongly Agree (7)

one-third of the responding managers agree that the increased competition within EU has resulted in lower overall prices in the Union. Although Europeans and non-Europeans alike have perceived the launch of the euro to be successful, the majority of respondents in this study also blame it for instigating a general increase in EU-wide prices.

Perhaps it is the price increases at home and the strength of euro internationally that has led to the suggestion by the responding EU managers that even the cost saving resulted from the consolidation of manufacturing and marketing across EU have not made EU manufacturers price competitive against their American counterparts. Indeed, of all pricing issues, the price-competitiveness of EU received the lowest (24.1%) level of agreement from the respondents. Even the scale economies due to the consolidation of manufacturing and marketing are not believed to have made the EU manufacturers more price-competitive globally. Furthermore, respondents actually believe that the euro has benefited US exporters by simplifying their international transactions and currency exchange needs. Ironically, this issue received the strongest support (61.5%) from the respondents.

Pricing Strategy

Even though the euro is blamed for price hikes across the euro-zone, it is also responsible for a shift in pricing strategy by the EU and non-EU companies. Almost half of the respondents suggest a shift towards EU-wide standard pricing strategy and nearly 40% of them suggest a single euro-zone price-positioning strategy by exporters. The ramifications of this uniform pricing strategy, regardless of the local demands, are significant. As one executive put it, while the standard pricing strategy has created a ". . . better transparency of pricing for consumers," with a single EU-wide price, ". . . the relationship between supply to each country and demand in that country is ignored–with a negative effect on profitability." In other words, parallel imports may be halted but with a uniform pricing strategy, the company may price itself out of the lower-end markets while not realizing its higher profit potentials in the higher-end EU economies.

As expected, respondents suggest that the move towards price uniformity is much stronger among the business and industrial manufacturers (46.3% agreement) than among the consumer goods suppliers (42.9% agreement). Again, as expected, respondents suggest that the pricing of services has not followed the same speed towards standardization even though price uniformity for the business and industrial services has more supporters than consumer services. Indeed, as one executive suggested ". . . I am in the investment banking industry–the euro has not had such an impact" which may be one reason behind the more sluggish move towards price uniformity in the services sector.

Distribution Issues

Distribution was expected to be the first major marketing area to be impacted by the formation of the European internal single market. (See Table 4.) Indeed, among all variables, it has achieved the highest level of Europeanization. On the retailing side, pan-European retailing has gained dominance and over two-thirds of respondents suggest that there has been a significant drop in the number of smaller retailers across EU. At the wholesale level, the respondents confirm what the marketing theory would indicate. Wholesale distributors have merged for efficiency, reducing the necessity for a large number of distributors to serve the European Union and diminishing the need for exclusive agents in the EU. Furthermore, cross-border cooperative buying by distributors and by

TABLE 3. Pricing Issues

Statement	Mean Score	Percent Agree*
Prices for consumer goods have become more uniform among EU countries.	3.67	42.9
Prices for consumer services have become more uniform among EU countries.	3.25	26.2
Prices for business and industrial products have become more uniform among EU countries.	4.05	46.3
Prices for business and industrial services have become more uniform among EU countries.	3.74	35.4
The euro has benefited US exporters since they now have to deal with only one currency across most of EU.	4.68	61.5
Products produced in the EU have become more price competitive globally, as a result of increased economies of scale.	3.86	36.7
Consolidation of manufacturing and marketing activities has made EU manufacturing companies as price-competitive as their US counterparts.	3.19	24.1
Successful introduction and acceptance of the euro has resulted in a shift towards standard pricing strategies across most EU countries.	4.07	49.4
Introduction of the euro resulted in a general price increase in the EU.	4.45	50.6
Many exporters to the EU use a single Euro-zone price position regardless of inter-EU demand differential.	4.06	38.8
Average prices in the EU have decreased due to increased competition.	3.75	33.7

*Statement equals Somewhat Agree (5), Agree (6) and Strongly Agree (7)

agents has increased and as one executive commented, ". . . we can negotiate with European wide retail/buying groups thereby leveraging European power to overcome weak country positions." As about one-half of the respondents suggest, all of this has resulted in faster and more efficient distribution services across Europe.

However, a surprising finding is the lack of significant support among the respondents on the issue of distribution costs. Similar to attitudes toward advertising and promotions, a minority (40%) of the executives responding to the survey believes that the overall distribution costs within the EU have dropped significantly. The cost savings resulting from consolidation and elimination of less efficient agents, reduction in bureaucracy and more efficient logistics may have been offset by increased global competition, trade promotions, higher retail margins, increasing labor costs and taxation. Indeed, only one-third of the respondents believes that integration of the EU markets has resulted in an overall drop in the overall corporate marketing costs.

TABLE 4. Distribution Issues

Statement	Mean Score	Percent Agree*
Pan-European retailing has become common.	4.35	51.2
Fewer distribution centers are now needed to serve the EU.	4.41	57.0
Compared to ten years ago, there has been a significant reduction in the number of smaller retailers.	4.81	67.7
Wholesale distributors have merged or consolidated to become more efficient.	4.39	52.2
Cross-border cooperative buying by dealers and distributors has increased.	4.69	64.9
The use of exclusive agents in the EU has diminished in importance.	4.09	46.3
Distribution services have become faster and more convenient.	4.43	50.0
Overall distribution costs within the EU have significantly dropped.	4.03	40.5

*Statement equals Somewhat Agree (5), Agree (6) and Strongly Agree (7)

Advertising and Promotion Issues

Executives in our sample definitely found many differences in advertising and promotion as a function of the internal market. (See Table 5.) Notably, they see the use of EU wide advertising campaigns (67.2%) and more focus on culturally based, rather than nationally based, advertising (58.4%). This has been notably led by changes in television advertising as the most effective traditional advertising medium (55.7%), which is seen as having changed to utilizing less language, and more visuals and music (65.8%) and the development of specialized channels to reach niche markets (63.0%). As a result, executives feel that the efficiency of advertising media buying has increased (56.7%). As an additional outcome, nearly half (49.3%) feel that advertising has become more strictly regulated.

CONCLUSIONS

The principal objective of this study was to address the impacts of Europe's internal market creation on strategic marketing decisions, as practiced by EU executives. Specifically, we aimed to delineate any marked movement towards a pan-European marketing strategy as exercised by EU companies over the period of 1993-2003. The results suggest that looking at the EU "from 10,000 meters high," this big picture

TABLE 5. Advertising and Promotion Issues

Statement	Mean Score	Percent Agree*
Standardized European advertising campaigns have become more widespread.	4.64	67.2
Efficiency of advertising media buying has increased.	4.15	56.7
Sales promotion costs (as a percent of sales) have decreased.	3.40	27.4
Advertising has become more strictly regulated.	4.26	49.3
Overall, more standardization of advertising media has resulted in reduced promotional costs as a percent of sales.	3.70	15.2
Television advertising has changed to utilize more visual cues and music and less speaking.	4.62	65.8
There has been less focus on national advertising within EU and more focus on "cultural-based" advertising campaigns targeting various cultures within EU countries.	4.44	58.4
Development of more specialized TV channels has led to targeting of smaller niche markets across the EU.	4.74	63.0
Use of television as an advertising medium increased significantly in the EU.	4.69	55.7
Use of radio as an advertising medium increased significantly in the EU.	3.80	33.2
Use of newspapers as an advertising medium increased significantly in the EU.	3.53	15.3
Use of magazines as an advertising medium increased significantly in the EU.	3.96	35.2
Use of outdoor as an advertising medium increased significantly in the EU.	3.91	26.1
Use of cinema as an advertising medium increased significantly in the EU.	3.46	19.1
Use of the Internet as an advertising medium increased significantly in the EU.	5.33	78.9

*Statement equals Somewhat Agree (5), Agree (6) and Strongly Agree (7)

shows a clear move towards unification, harmonization and integration of marketing strategy across Europe.

Product strategy, in particular, appears to have been clearly impacted by the EU formation. As the executives surveyed noted, product availability and variety across the EU has improved; Euro branding has become commonplace; and overall product quality has been enhanced. Furthermore, as expected, the creation of a single market has led to centralized manufacturing leading to scale economies and efficiency in production for Euro-companies. Nevertheless, somewhat surprisingly, over the past decade, the rate of product innovation has not increased nor has EU-wide, single product positioning generally materialized. Perhaps the significant cultural differences within the EU can partly explain the latter while the former is puzzling especially in lieu of the increased competition with the EU.

Advertising and promotion practices have moved towards integration and standardization. According to the responding executives, corporate advertising has moved from a national-based to a cultural-based mode before making its move towards a more Europe-wide approach. Television media has gained dominance in the EU, with TV ads evolving from being more cultural language-based to more universal visuals and music-based themes. Similar to the United States, the EU television environment has changed as well, with many niche channels carrying specialized and highly targeted ads towards their potential target markets. As expected, consolidations have resulted in a rise in the efficiency of advertising media buying in the European Union.

What is surprising, however, is the strong belief by the executives that their advertising and promotional expenses (as a percentage of sales) have not declined, given the standardization and consolidation that has taken place over the past decade. There are a number of reasons for this outcome. First, even though efficiencies in advertising have been achieved, due to the increased competition for media and the move towards more costly media (e.g., TV), overall advertising and promotion budgets have not necessarily declined. Second, the competitive landscape in Europe has changed, which has led to the need for more aggressive advertising campaigns within the union and abroad. Third, many companies have maintained a fixed ad-sales ratio over the long run.

Distribution was expected to benefit the most from the single market creation, partly due to the massive bureaucratic legal and inefficient infrastructure in Europe, and the executives surveyed in general agree with this proposition, widely espoused by academicians. In general, pan-European retailing has gained dominance and smaller retailers have been eliminated or absorbed. Wholesalers have become larger through mergers, acquisitions or alliances, have become more efficient, and have gained more power in dealing with manufacturers and other channel members. Nevertheless, the respondents in our study are still not strongly committed to the premise that all those efficiencies have led to a reduction in their distribution costs. Perhaps competition has resulted in more costly trade promotion strategies, larger sales forces, or higher margins for retailers and brokers. Given the results from the above discussion, it is not surprising that the respondents do not strongly support the academic expectation that the single market creation would lead to a reduction in overall marketing costs.

Price is the one element of the marketing mix that has generated the most "surprises," compared to academic expectations. The executives surveyed do not strongly support what academics take as a given, specifically, that increased competition would lead to a general trend towards lower prices, especially when production efficiencies are achieved. The euro has not helped in that matter, either. Indeed, the executives attribute the lack of downward pressure on EU-wide prices partly to the strength of the euro. Furthermore, it is suggested that the single market creation and the successful introduction of the euro has not made EU companies more price-competitive globally. What is comforting, however, is the executives' confirmation of pan-European pricing strategy and EU-wide price positioning. Price harmonization is, as expected, taking place faster in the industrial sector and overall, the prices of manufactured goods are more harmonized than those of services.

In short, the results suggest an overall trend towards a standard pan-European marketing strategy with some elements of the marketing mix lagging behind. The future appears to be on the side of uniformity with some allowance for cultural differences. This exploratory study definitely suggests the need for further investigation into the actual effect of the EU internal market on marketing and business strategy and tactics.

REFERENCES

Baalbaki, Imad and Naresh K. Malhotra (1995), "Standardization versus Customization in International Marketing: An Investigation Using Bridging Conjoint Analysis," *Journal of the Academy of Marketing Science*, 23 (3), pp 182-194.

Berns-Wright, Linda and Fred W. Morgan (2002), "Comparative advertising in the European Union and the United States: Legal and managerial issues," *Journal of Euromarketing*, Vol. 11, No. 3, pp 7-31.

Blanco, Jose (2001), "The Euro as an opportunity for value creation," *Managerial Finance*, Vol. 27, No. 9, pp 41-53.

Boddewyn, Jean and Robert Grosse (1995), "American marketing in the European Union: Standardization's uneven progress (1973-1993)," *European Journal of Marketing*, Vol. 29, No. 12, pp 23-42.

Diamantopoulos, A., B. Schlegelmilch and J. Du Preez (1995), "Lessons for pan-European Marketing? The role of consumer preferences in fine-tuning the product-market fit," *International Marketing Review*, Vol. 12, No. 2, pp 38-52.

Dowling, Bob (2002), "Who Really Speaks for Europe," *Business Week*, November 25, p 70.

Ganesh, Jaishankar (1998), "Converging trends within the European Union: Insights from an analysis of diffusion patterns," *Journal of International Marketing*, Volume 6, Number 4, pp 32-48.

Hildebrand, Doris (1994), "Legal aspects of Euro-marketing," *European Journal of Marketing*, Volume 28, No. 7, pp 44-54.

Hofstede, Frenkel ter, Michel Wedel and Steenkamp and Jan-Benedict (2002), "Identifying Spatial Segments in International Markets," *Marketing Science*, Vol. 21, No. 2, pp 160-177.

Jain, Subbash (1989), "Standardization of International Marketing Strategy: Some Research Hypotheses," *Journal of Marketing*, Vol. 53 (January), pp 70-79.

Jakubowski, Irena (1995), "Pan-European Marketing," *British Food Journal*, Volume 97, No. 6, pp 18.

Jallat, Frederic and Allan J. Kimmel (2002), "Marketing in culturally diverse environments: The case of Western Europe," *Business Horizons*, Vol. 45, No. 4, (Jul/Aug), pp 30-36.

Kale, Sudhir (1995), "Grouping Euroconsumers: A culture-based clustering approach," *Journal of International Marketing*, Vol. 3, No. 3, pp 35-49.

Kouremenos, Athanassios and George Avlonitis (1995), "The changing consumer in Greece," *International Journal of Research in Marketing*, Vol. 12, Issue 5 (December), pp 435-448.

Leeflang, Peter and Fred van Raaij (1995), "The changing consumer in the European Union: A 'meta-analysis,'" *International Journal of Research in Marketing*, Vol. 12, Issue 5 (December), pp 373-387.

Levitt, Theodore (1983), "The Globalization of Markets," *Harvard Business Review*, Vol. 61, pp 92-102.

McGowan, Lee (1998), "Protecting Competition in a Global Market: The Pursuit of an International Competition Policy," *European Business Review*, Volume 98, No. 6, pp 328-339.

Norman, Peter (2002), "Europe Reinvented," Part 1, *Financial Times*, pp 4.

Petty, Ross (1997), "Advertising law in the United States and European Union," *Journal of Public Policy and Marketing*, (Spring), pp 2-13.

Poist, Richard F., Carl Scheraga and Janjaap Semeijn (2001), "Preparation of Logistics Managers for the Contemporary Environment of the European Union," *International Journal of Physical Distribution and Logistics Management*, Vol. 31, No. 7/8, pp 287-504.

Reilly, Tom (1995), "The harmonization of standards in the European Union and the impact on U.S. business," *Business Horizon*, Volume 38, Issue 2 (March-April), pp 28-34.

Saghafi, M., D. Sciglimpaglia and B. Withers (1995), "Strategic Decisions for American and European Industrial Marketers in a Unified European Market," *Industrial Marketing Management*, (March), pp 69-81.

Steenkamp and Hofstede (1999), "A Cross-National Investigation into the Individual and National Cultural Antecedents of Consumer Innovativeness," *Journal of Marketing*, Vol. 63, No. 2, pp 55-69.

Steinert, Bruce (1998), "Harmonisation: International Rules Coming to a Planet Near You," *SRA Journal* (Summer/Fall), pp 69-71.

Seitz, Victoria (1998), "Direct response advertising in the US and European Markets: A Content Analysis of Fashion Products," *European Business Review*, Vol. 98, No. 5, pp 268-275.

Thorne-LeClair, Debbie, O. Farrell and L. Farrell (1997), "Federal Sentencing Guidelines for Organizations: Legal, Ethical and Public Policy Issues for International Marketing," *Journal of Public Policy and Marketing* (Spring), pp 26-37.

Thorne-LeClair, Debbie (2000), "Marketing Planning and the Policy Environment in the European Union," *International Marketing Review*, Vol. 17, No. 3, pp 193-215.

Wall Street Journal (2000), "Microsoft's Problem in EU," April 6, p 1.

Whitelock, Jeryl and Carole Pimblett (1997), "The Standardization Debate in International Marketing," *Journal of Global Marketing*, Vol. 10, No. 3, pp 45-66.

Wierenga, Berend, Ad Pruyn and Eric Waarts (1996), "The key to successful Euromarketing: Standardization or customization?" *Journal of International Consumer Marketing*, Vol. 8, No. 3-4, pp 39-67.

Will, George (1997), "European Fudging," *Newsweek*, June 23, pp 84.

Marketing Practice and Market Orientation: An Exploratory International Study

Roger Palmer

Jaqueline Pels

SUMMARY. Despite the criticism of the role of marketing in the firm, a market-oriented corporate culture is considered as a key element of superior corporate performance, with many studies demonstrating this linkage. A recent study by Matsuno and Mentzer (2000) considers the effect of strategy type on the relationship between market orientation and corporate performance. However, these linkages between market orientation, strategic stance and corporate performance are by no means clear-cut. This paper argues that generic measures of strategy implementation are at too high a level of abstraction. The current study proposes that the CMP (Contemporary Marketing Practice)[1] typology of marketing practice, which explains a wide range of relationship marketing approaches, provides greater insight into the relationship between market orientation and performance.

Various studies have suggested that market orientation influences business performance. It is proposed that business performance is too coarse a measure of the influence of the type of marketing practice. Marketing outcomes are proposed as intervening between marketing practice and corporate performance.

Roger Palmer is affiliated with Cranfield School of Management, Cranfield, Bedford MK43 7ER, UK (E-mail: r.a.palmer@cranfield.ac.uk). Jaqueline Pels is affiliated with Universidad Torcuato Di Tella, Miñones 2159, Buenos Aires, Argentina (E-mail: jaquie@mail.retina.ar).

[Haworth co-indexing entry note]: "Marketing Practice and Market Orientation: An Exploratory International Study." Palmer, Roger, and Jaqueline Pels. Co-published simultaneously in *Journal of Euromarketing* (International Business Press, an imprint of The Haworth Press, Inc.) Vol. 14, No. 1/2, 2004, pp. 59-86; and: *Marketing Issues in Western Europe: Changes and Developments* (eds: Erdener Kaynak, and Frédéric Jallat) International Business Press, an imprint of The Haworth Press, Inc., 2004, pp. 59-86. Single or multiple copies of this article are available for a fee from The Haworth Document Delivery Service [1-800-HAWORTH, 9:00 a.m. - 5:00 p.m. (EST). E-mail address: docdelivery@haworthpress.com].

In addition, in this study we investigate further the role of turbulence as a moderator of market orientation by gathering comparative data from Argentina and the UK.

These discussions are summarised by a theoretical model and a series of theoretical propositions. The study seeks to test and refine these propositions as the output of this study and as the basis for further work. *[Article copies available for a fee from The Haworth Document Delivery Service: 1-800-HAWORTH. E-mail address: <docdelivery@haworthpress.com> Website: <http://www.HaworthPress.com> © 2004 by The Haworth Press, Inc. All rights reserved.]*

KEYWORDS. Market orientation, developing economies, contemporary marketing practice, relationship marketing, transaction marketing, cluster analysis

INTRODUCTION

Despite the criticism of the role of marketing in the firm (Brady and Davis, 1993), a market-oriented corporate culture is considered as a key element of superior corporate performance, with many studies demonstrating this linkage (see, for example, Homburg and Pflesser, 2000). Though market orientation-corporate performance and the market orientation-corporate performance relationship are defined differently by various authors, the importance of the core link has been recognised in many conceptual and empirical studies. Kohli and Jaworski (1990), Jaworski and Kohli (1993), Narver and Slater (1990) proposed different market orientation models that allow the operationalization of the concept of market orientation. Since the initial work of the early 90s, the market orientation-corporate performance link has been enriched by the investigation of various modifiers of the relationship, such as the role of strategy and environmental turbulence.

A recent study by Matsuno and Mentzer (2000) considers the effect of strategy type on the relationship between market orientation and corporate performance. However these linkages between market orientation, strategic stance and corporate performance are by no means clear-cut. This paper argues that generic measures of strategy implementation are at too high a level of abstraction, and that more sensitive measures of company performance are required. The current study has been conducted by members of the Contemporary Marketing Practice group (CMP),[2] and proposes that the CMP typology of marketing practice offers the opportunity for greater insight into the relationship between market orientation and performance.

In addition, performance needs to be considered not just in relation to market orientation but also to the environment in which the firms operate. With regard to the role of environmental turbulence, work reported by Gatignon and Xuereb (1997) and Homburg and Pflesser (2000) suggests that market orientation results in improved performance in conditions of environmental uncertainty. However, other work has noted discrepancies between the various instruments used to determine market orientation. For example Uncles (2000), proposes turbulence as a moderator of market orientation supported by the empirical work of Homburg and Pflesser (2000), while market orientation was not seen by Greenley (1995) to be advantageous in highly turbulent markets. This paper proposes that these deductive approaches, attempting to measure the relationship between variables and identify causes of variance, are unlikely to ever offer a complete explanation of the role of market orientation in different contexts. In this study, we use an inductive approach to investigate further the role of turbulence as a moderator of market orientation by using comparative data from Argentina and the UK.

We propose that there is a multiplicity of variables that are difficult to measure, or are capable of being measured in alternative and possibly non-commensurate ways. By focusing to variables and the relationship between variables the argument can potentially descend into a discussion of definition and measurement. In this way the insight possible from a broader understanding of context can be lost in the detail of debate. In this paper we propose to consider these areas from an alternative methodological perspective in order to gain greater insight.

Various forms of evidence from Argentina and the UK are used in order to test a model that represents an understanding of the mechanisms taking place, rather than to statistically explore the relationship between variables. The study seeks to test a number of theoretical propositions and to refine them as the output of this study and as the basis for further work.

In particular, the paper explores the relationship between market orientation, environmental turbulence, marketing stance as demonstrated by CMP derived typologies, market served, marketing outcomes and corporate performance. We first review the literature concerning the moderators and variables (market orientation, strategy, environmental turbulence and corporate performance). We then explain the methodology used and introduce the theoretical model and related theoretical propositions. We present and discuss the data and close with the conclusions and suggestions for further research.

MEASURING MARKET ORIENTATION

Uncles (2000) states that market orientation *"is concerned with the processes and activities associated with creating and satisfying customers by continually assessing their needs and wants, and doing so in a way that there is a demonstrable and measurable impact on business performance."* Market orientation is therefore a component of the overall business strategy, which is seen to contribute positively to business performance.

With a number of different measures for market orientation this also raises the question of which scale most appropriately measures this construct. The original MARKOR scale by Kohli and Jaworski (1990) has been supplemented by others and the debate continues as to which is the most appropriate (Bhuian, 1998; Mavondo and Farrell, 2000).

The Kohli and Jaworski (MARKOR) and Narver and Slater (1990) (MKTOR) models are generally regarded as comparable in terms of output, and have been widely used by other researchers. However, the similarities in reported results belie differences in the detail of the instruments themselves. The Kohli and Jaworski framework considers the generation and dissemination of market intelligence and the associated organisational response. The Narver and Slater model considers cultural underpinnings in addition to the behavioural elements of customer orientation, competitor orientation and inter-functional co-ordination. When considering the choice of instrument to use, validity is a primary concern. This is particularly the case with respect to the study reported here, due to the international nature of the study and the widely varying environmental contexts.

Mavondo and Farrell (2000) argue for the Narver and Slater instrument as being more appropriate for cross-cultural, cross-country, cross-group and cross-industry comparisons of market orientation. However, their study was conducted solely within the context of the Australian market and primarily compared business with consumer markets. Uncles (2000) notes that three other papers reporting cross-country findings, and appearing in the same special edition of a journal dedicated to the subject, did not use the MKTOR instrument. Bhuian (1998) is also critical of the Kohli and Jaworski MARKOR instrument, arguing that it reflected behaviours rather than understandings. By contrast, Sigauw and Diamantopoulos (1995) propose that there are shortcomings in the MKTOR scale of Narver and Slater. Uncles (2000) is less definitive with respect to the Kohli and Jaworski instrument but argues for more work on this topic.

Dawes (2000) proposes the view that the various measures of market orientation are composed of aggregate measures. He proposes that it is possible to consider the individual components of each of the various instruments that are available, citing the work of Greenley (1995) whose work suggests different expressions of market orientation reflecting different component parts of the instruments. In addition, exploratory factor analysis showed that the single factor explained only a relatively low proportion of the variance. This therefore provides justification to the various studies that use one or other instruments updated in the light of further work or the circumstances of the study (e.g., Matsuno and Mentzer, 2000; Homburg and Pflesser, 2000).

However, perhaps the biggest shortcoming that Dawes identified in his review of thirty-six studies conducted between 1992-98, is that all but one were cross-sectional in design. He proposes that as a result claims for causality are less robust and that the lagged effect of certain time dependent variables cannot be determined (Bollen, 1989). Overall, this debate is far from closed, both MKTOR and MARKOR have their advocates and critics, and currently there is no agreed standard market orientation measurement. In the absence of consensus on this issue, our use of the MARKOR scale is justified below.

The study reported in this paper uses the original measure of market orientation devised by Kohli and Jaworski, the MARKOR instrument. A modified Kohli and Jaworski scale was used by Matsuno and Mentzer (2000) and their paper serves as a framework against which this study has been developed. The literature review of Olsen (2001) identified that this scale, or modifications thereof, was more commonly used in international studies, particularly with regard to South American countries. The Kohli and Jaworski instrument was therefore used in order to maintain face comparability with other data generated from the Argentine locus of the study.

IMPLEMENTED STRATEGY

Walker and Ruekert (1987) discuss business level strategy as the linkage between the external environment and the firm. Market orientation is one construct that helps to explain this linkage. However, researchers in the area of market orientation commonly adapt scales and seek moderating variables in order to further explain variance. Matsuno and Mentzer (2000) consider the role of business strategy type on the market orientation-corporate performance relationship. The results of their study demonstrated the modifying effect of business strategy.

If strategy represents the relationship between the firm and the external business environment (Miles and Snow, 1978), and market orientation is a subset of that strategy, then this implies that there are many other potential variables and moderating factors that can complicate the understanding of this relationship. For example, this is discussed by Greenley (1995), who investigates the role of moderating variables and questions the positive linkage implicitly assumed between market orientation and business performance, identifying circumstances in which this relationship is unlikely to hold.

The way that we understand strategy can also be questioned. Does this refer to the formulated marketing strategy or the strategy that is implemented? (Mintzberg, 1994; Menon, Bharadaj, Adidam and Edison, 1999). How can this strategy be characterised and does it truly reflect marketing activity, or does it also encompass other aspects of the firm's behaviour? These could include sound financial control or excellence in production and resource management compensating for otherwise indifferent marketing strategy.

This study takes as its basis that of Matsuno and Mentzer (2000), although the methodology employed is very different. Matsuno and Mentzer consider the moderating effect of the type of strategy on the linkage between market orientation and business performance. In this study, we argue that actual or realised marketing strategy is more closely reflective of a market orientation, and is subject to fewer moderating variables compared to a more coarse-grained reflection of business strategy. Matsuno and Mentzer used the strategy typologies defined by Miles and Snow (1978). The study has progressed by using the Contemporary Marketing Practice instrument that reflects realised marketing strategy, rather than strategy at the level of the firm.

Building on the use of strategy typologies, the study reported in this paper has used a typology of marketing practice developed by the Contemporary Marketing Practice (CMP) group of researchers (Brodie, Coviello, Brookes and Little, 1997; Coviello, Milley and Marcolin, 2001). The CMP typology has several potential advantages in a study of this nature. It represents a finer-grained definition of marketing strategy, as compared to strategy at the level of the firm. It therefore offers the potential to give greater insight into the linkage between market orientation and performance, with less unexplained variance due to other moderating variables.

Conceptualizing Contemporary Marketing Practice

According to a number of academics, firms are now emphasizing the retention of customers and the management of relationships, where relationships extend beyond the buyer-seller dyad to include partners through the value chain (Day and Montgomery, 1999; Morgan and Hunt, 1994; Webster, 1992). This approach to the market is generally referred to as relationship marketing, and has been defined by Morgan and Hunt (1994, p. 34) as ". . . all marketing activities directed towards establishing, developing, and maintaining successful relational exchanges."

The relational view of marketing has evolved from efforts by both business-to-business (Hakansson, 1982; Hakansson and Snehota, 1995) and services scholars (Berry, 1983; Christopher, Payne and Ballantyne, 1991; Gummesson, Lehtinen and Grönroos, 1997) to differentiate marketing practices by the nature of the customer served or product offered. Beyond the business-to-business and services arenas however, there are also theoretical developments pertaining to consumer markets and goods firms, thus extending the relevance of relationships across different contexts (Pels, 1999; Sheth and Parvatiyar, 1995). Given this evolution, one might argue that any understanding of "contemporary" marketing should include the concept of relationships, and this is reflected in the argument that relationship marketing offers a new paradigm for the field (Sheth, Gardner and Garrett, 1988; Webster, 1992). For example, in his review of the changing role of marketing in the corporation, Webster (1992) outlines an extended continuum of marketing relationships, and argues for a new paradigm of the marketing function in the firm. Similarly, Berry (1983) identifies different forms or levels of relational marketing, thus suggesting a continuum in terms of the range of relationship-building practices that might be implemented. A third continuum is offered by Grönroos (1990), who argues that the nature of the product offer and the type of customer served impacts how a firm relates to its market. He proposes that consumer packaged goods organizations are normally characterized by transaction marketing and dominated by the marketing mix. Slightly less transactional and more relational practices are expected for consumer durable and industrial goods firms. Service organizations are posited to be at the relational end of the continuum.

The CMP group argues that a more pluralistic conceptualization of marketing is required and Coviello, Brodie and Munro developed a first classification in 1997. This first classification was later refined in 2001 by Coviello, Milley and Marcolin (see Appendix A). This framework does not view transactional and relational marketing to be separate paradigms, mutually exclusive, or at opposite ends of a continuum. Rather, it suggests that marketing is characterized by multiple complex processes manifested in five different aspects of marketing practice (Coviello, Brodie, Brookes and Palmer, 2003):

Transaction Marketing–involves a firm attracting and satisfying potential buyers by managing the elements of the marketing mix, whereby the seller actively manages communication "to" buyers in a mass-market in order to create discrete, arms-length transactions.

Database Marketing–involves using a database technology to create a type of relationship, thus allowing firms to compete in a manner different from mass marketing. The intent is to retain identified customers although marketing is still "to" the customer, rather than "with" the customer. Relationships as such are not close or interpersonal, and are facilitated and personalised through the use of database technology.

Interaction Marketing–implies face-to-face interaction between individuals. As such, it is truly "with" the customer, as both parties invest resources to develop a mutually beneficial and interpersonal relationship.

Network Marketing–occurs across organisations, where managers commit resources to develop the firm's position in a network of firm level relationships.

E-Marketing–the latest marketing practice to be characterised by the group, is defined as using the internet and other interactive technologies to create and mediate dialogue between the firm and identified customers.

The nature of the multiple processes can be investigated further by means of cluster analysis, using the Transaction Marketing, Database Marketing, Interaction Marketing, Network Marketing and E-Marketing construct scores to group the firms in terms of their marketing practice profile. The clusters were formed using k-means cluster analysis. The number of clusters was varied between one and six, resulting finally in a 3-cluster solution (see Table 4) on the basis of the average within-cluster difference criterion (Hair et al., 1998). The first cluster has an above average score for Transaction Marketing, but is well below average on the Database Marketing, Interaction Marketing, E-Marketing and Network Marketing constructs. It is, therefore, a cluster largely comprised of firms practicing Transaction Marketing. The second cluster has above average construct scores for all five marketing practice constructs. This might be termed a "Transactional/Relational" cluster since these firms practice high levels of all marketing approaches. The third and final cluster is above average on Interaction Marketing, E-Marketing and Network Marketing and well below average on Transaction Marketing and Database Marketing. Hence, this is called a "Relational" cluster on the basis of its bias towards Interaction and Network Marketing. Overall, there are three clearly defined clusters.

Thus, a well-validated instrument is used to gather data from co-operating companies and this can be analysed to develop an understanding of the respondents marketing practices.

GENERAL AND MARKET ENVIRONMENT

Many authors studying the relationship between market orientation and business performance have acknowledged that the link is affected or modified by a number of environmental factors (Miller, 1987; Kohli and Jaworski, 1990; Greenley, 1995).

Unfortunately, there is no consensus as to the precise meaning of the term environment. Kohli and Jaworski (1990) suggested three environmental moderators–technology turbulence, industry competition and the effect of the general economy. While Miller (1987) defines environment as market turbulence, explained as the influence of changing customer needs on marketing operations.

Furthermore, there is no consensus as to the effect or impact of these modifiers on the market orientation-corporate performance relation. In their 1993 study Jaworski and Kohli concluded that *"the market orientation of a business is an important determinant of its performance, regardless of the market turbulence, competitive intensity, or the technological turbulence of the environment in which it operates."* However, Greenley (1995) suggested that market orientation might not be advantageous in highly turbulent markets. Interestingly, in their 1996 article, Selnes, Jaworski and Kohli conclude that research on the relationship between external environmental factors and market orientation is of particular interest.

This leaves us in the situation of having to decide whether or not to include an environmental modifier and how to measure it. Our study was strongly motivated by the statement of Kohli, Jaworski and Kumar (1993) *"it will be interesting to see if the positive effects of market orientation on performance generalise to non-US economies. This will be particularly interesting in developing economies."* Consequently, we decided to review the literature and studies related to emerging markets. It is important to note that most of the studies in this field have been conducted in developed economies. A literature review shows that of forty studies considering market orientation and corporate performance only five were conducted in transition or emerging economies (Golden, Doney, Johnson and Smith, 1995; Pitt, Carauna and Berthon, 1996; Martin, Martin and Gbrac, 1998).

None of these reached decisive conclusions on the role of the environment. Having no clear evidence that the impact of an environmental modifier could be ruled out, we have decided to include this variable. Given the nature of our study, comparing an emerging economy experiencing high levels of market and general economic turbulence (Argentina) with a developed and stable economy (UK), our focus will be on the impact of the general economy (Kohli and Jaworski, 1990) on the market orientation-corporate performance relation.

BUSINESS PERFORMANCE

An additional factor discussed here relates to business performance. This is a multifactorial construct that can potentially be measured in many different ways. Does it relate for example to profitability this year, or over a period of time, growth in market share, customer retention—or all or none of these? There is an explicit assumption that a market orientation improves business performance. However, defining and measuring business performance can be problematic, as this may depend upon the objectives of the organisation (Bititci, 1994).

Narver and Slater (1990) considered performance in terms of profitability, and more specifically return on assets. The use of single items as measures of corporate performance poses a number of problems (Pelham, 1997). These could include obtaining information on company performance due to confidentiality, differences in accounting and financial procedures and problems in obtaining comparable competitor data (Styles, 1998; Hartenian and Gudmundson, 2000). Therefore it is desirable to obtain data from a variety of sources.

Objective, independently verifiable, data *per se* can be unreliable as evidenced by the increasing questioning of reported accounting data. Therefore subjective, relative or interpretive data may be both more accessible than absolute/objective data and more appropriate. Geringer and Herbert (1991) and Dess and Robinson (1984) demonstrate that subjective performance measures can be strongly correlated with objective data. Venkataraman and Ramanajam (1986) also show that perceptual data gives acceptable feedback on business and economic performance.

With respect to the context of the study undertaken, reliance upon objective data is further complicated when collecting data in transition economies such as Argentina. The type and magnitude of the data can vary depending on the target audience, tax authorities for example, and multiple accounting records are often maintained (Olsen, 2001). In these circumstances subjective measures as reported by respondents may prove more reliable than objective data.

The CMP group in developing their instrument has used a number of subjective measures (Coviello et al., 2002). The criteria offered in the CMP questionnaire, following Homburg and Plesser (2000) included: sales growth, new customer gain, customer retention, profitability, customer satisfaction and achievement of market share, as well as the option "other." In formulating this element of the questionnaire, guidelines from the literature have also been followed. For example, using relative rather than absolute figures to report change (Homburg and Pflesser, 2000), measuring performance relative to primary competitors (Matsuno and Mentzer, 2000) and against expectations and objectives.

In order to more closely investigate the linkage between market orientation and marketing strategy, we therefore consider not general business performance indicators, but those relating to markets, in particular, sales growth. Again, this is an attempt to focus to those factors more specifically influenced by marketing as opposed to general business strategy. We refer to these as marketing outcomes (MOt). The subjective measures of business performance incorporated within the contemporary marketing practice instrument are also used.

THEORETICAL MODEL AND PROPOSITIONS

The role of the model is to represent the structures and underlying mechanisms that loosely govern the relationship between the elements from which the model is constructed (Blaikie, 1993). The model can then be empirically tested against the data and the output of this process can then be used to refine the model. A model is usually accompanied by a series of propositions concerning relationships between the concepts captured within the model (Figure 1).

As this is a unique and exploratory study, the context imposes a constraint as to the level of generalisability, the test for such a model is not proof, but plausibility. This is tested against a broader community of scholars and, hence, peer review is important in order to test the rigour of the work and the degree to which the findings are credible (Hirschman, 1986). This work has been discussed within the CMP group and has also been the subject of various conference papers. The theoretical propositions that accompany the model are discussed below, these are tested against the results of the study and, in this way, theory can be developed further.

In circumstances of turbulence, it could be argued that factors other than marketing practice, such as the extent of indebtedness and ability to control costs, could be more important to business survival than marketing practice. In more stable markets that are more predictable, then differentiation through more relational marketing practices may be more important. Stability and predictability are consistent with market

FIGURE 1. Theoretical Model

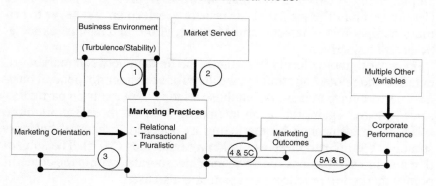

maturity and hence product parity. We propose that differentiation via relational practices may be more important in such circumstances.

Theoretical proposition 1: *Firms in developed markets adopt relational marketing practices in comparison to firms in turbulent markets.*

Previous work by the CMP group has shown that the context of the business influences the type of marketing practice. This theoretical proposition seeks to test further the validity of this finding.

Theoretical proposition 2: *That marketing practice will vary by the profile of the market served.*

This argues that a higher level of market orientation, a strategic factor as discussed previously, will be associated with relational marketing practice, arguably a richer approach to marketing requiring a higher degree of expertise (Gummesson, 2000). Market orientated firms will therefore be more capable in the practice of marketing.

Theoretical proposition 3: *That a higher degree of market orientation will be associated with relational marketing practice.*

A number of different marketing typologies have been identified that represent different types of marketing practice. Several relationship marketing authors (Grönroos, 1992; Hakansson and Snehota, 1995; Holmlund, 1997; Gummesson, 2000) have argued that relationship marketers should be using different performance measurements such as customer satisfaction, customer retention, return-on-relationship, etc. This theoretical proposition seeks to investigate whether or not these practices seek to achieve different outcomes.

Theoretical proposition 4: *That different marketing typologies will be associated with different measures of marketing outcomes.*

Theoretical propositions 5A and 5B explore the view previously discussed that firm performance is too coarse a measure and is composed of too many variables to give a meaningful indication of the influence on performance of marketing practice. By considering marketing outcomes as a finer grained view of marketing rather than corporate performance, these propositions seek to build an explanation between, marketing practice, marketing outcomes and firm performance. Theoretical proposition 5C suggests that the more proficient and diverse a firm is at the practice of marketing, then the greater the reward that accrues in terms of marketing outcomes.

Theoretical proposition 5A: *That firm performance is not associated with the typology of marketing practice.*

Theoretical proposition 5B: *That marketing outcomes are associated with the typology of marketing practice.*

Theoretical proposition 5C: *That relational and pluralistic marketing practices will deliver higher levels of marketing outcomes.*

METHODOLOGY

The research programme has a limited respondent base with sparse or absent data in certain categories. For this reason, the research is positioned as an exploratory project, however, we believe the work is important as it is revelatory, in that a comparison of this nature between a transitional and developed economy has not previously been conducted. Within the overall methodology two main methods have been used to gather data. Primarily using the CMP questionnaire, but general information about the respondents' environment is presented to give an understanding of context.

The project has been conducted from a realist rather than positivist perspective. The primary purpose from this perspective is to give insight and understanding, rather than to discover a truth by proving the relationship between variables. From this perspective, the limitations imposed by the data are less constraining as, whilst a theoretical model is presented, this is intended to suggest the overall mechanism, rather than to demonstrate the specific relationships between variables. From a realist perspective, events are not seen as being directly and causally linked, as would be the case from a positivist perspective and for which more complete data would be required, but are contextually dependent. It is the search for underlying mechanisms that leads to insight and understanding. The realist perspective is commensurate with this revelatory, inductive approach (Easton, 1995).

A self-administered questionnaire was used to operationalise the classification of marketing typologies. In addition, data were collected about each firm's customer base, marketing practices and organisational details. The CMP protocol was again adopted for this programme of research, full details of which are discussed in Coviello, Brodie, Danaher and Johnston (2002). Accordingly we used a convenience sample of managers participating in MBA programmes taught by members of the research team based in Argentina and the UK. In total, 119 responses (Argentina, 67, UK, 52) were suitable for analysis. Predominantly responses were obtained from business to business services firm (Argentina, 32, UK, 30). Other types of firms were well represented in the Argentine data, but in the UK sample only 2 firms were classed as being in the consumer goods category (Table 1).

The UK managers had an average age of 31 and 7 years work experience, most had tertiary qualifications and had held middle/senior management positions. The Argentinean managers had a similar profile, with an average age of 30. They were, thus, considered to be well qualified to comment on marketing issues. This type of sample is consistent with other international studies (Neelankavil, Mathur and Zhang, 2000).

In addition to the survey questions, respondents were given the opportunity to contribute qualitative comments that further enriched understanding. The survey instrument was in English, and all respondents were either native speakers or highly proficient in the language. Participants were briefed to carefully consider the questions and to discuss them with colleagues within their own organisations and to use a variety of data sources accessible to them. Respondents were told of the nature of study, but data collection took place before the start of the formal teaching programme in order to minimise exposure to marketing theory and potential bias. The results of the survey were analysed using SPSS.

TABLE 1. Firms Within Sample by Business Sector–% of Sample

	Argentina	UK
Business to Consumer ~ Goods	18	7
Business to Business ~ Goods	19	18
Business to Consumer ~ Services	19	18
Business to Business ~ Services	38	38
Other (i.e., Not for Profit)	6	19
Total	*100*	*100*

DATA AND RESULTS

Context

An important attribute of the methodology adopted is that it enables the phenomenon to be understood within context. Table 2 summarises comparative data from Argentina and the UK, drawn from a range of sources, to demonstrate the contrast between turbulent and stable economic environments. It can clearly be seen that Argentina exemplifies turbulence, whilst the UK represents a stable economic environment. The survey was conducted a few months before the onset of the economic crisis that Argentina experienced from late 2001.

Contemporary Marketing Practice

Table 3 shows the results of the SPSS analysis from both the Argentine and UK samples. The CMP typologies of marketing practice are cross tabulated against the results of a cluster analysis. Following the work of Coviello et al. (2002), a cluster analysis was undertaken in order to abstract the data to a higher level of analysis. Table 4 illustrates the results of a three cluster analysis. Each cluster has been named to illustrate the key characteristics of transactional, relational and pluralistic marketing.

Averaging the scores for a range of constructs used to measure each practice derives the scores noted in Table 3. These are scored on a 1 (low) to 5 (high) scale; the average is then divided by 5 to arrive at a (0) low to 1 (high) average score for each practice consistent with other CMP studies (Coviello et al., 2002). The highest scores for the transactional and relational clusters are represented in bold to demonstrate

TABLE 2. Economic Performance Indicators–Argentina and UK–1991-2001

		1991	1997	1998	1999	2000	2001 qtr 1	2001 qtr 2	2001 qtr 3	2001 qtr 4
% Unemployment	Arg	6.9	16.1	13.2	14.5	15.4	14.7	16.4	-	-
	UK	8.2	6.9	6.1	5.9	5.5	-	-	-	5.2
GDP % growth	Arg	-	8.1	3.9	−3.4	−.05	−6.9	−1.1	-	-
	UK	-	3.4	3.0	2.1	2.9	-	-	-	1.9
Deposit Rate #	Arg	-	6.99	7.57	8.08	8.4	8.5	13.5	27.7	-
	UK	11.85	6.62	7.35	5.34	5.97	6.00	5.30	5.0	-

Sources: Adapted from Indec, Bord and Assocs, www.moneyextra.com, NSO.
Arg–Annual average of monthly interest rates, UK–Annual average base rate.

TABLE 3. Marketing Practice and Typologies

CMP ~ practice	Transactional		Relational		Pluralistic	
	Arg (N = 14)	UK (N = 7)	Arg (N = 19)	UK (N = 17)	Arg (N = 22)	UK (N = 31)
Transactional Marketing	**.78**	**.81**	.53	.62	**.71**	**.67**
Direct Marketing	.57	.53	.48	.52	**.61**	**.64**
E-Marketing	.46	.48	.41	.47	**.64**	**.63**
Interaction Marketing	.50	.48	**.78**	**.75**	**.78**	**.77**
Network Marketing	.51	.51	.59	.55	**.62**	**.71**

the linkage between the practice and the cluster. The pluralistic cluster demonstrates above average (0.5) scores on each practice and hence demonstrates that the respondent companies concurrently practice a range of marketing styles.

Consistent with previous CMP, studies scores above 0.75 reflect higher levels of marketing practice; scores between 0.60 and 0.75 reflect medium levels of marketing practice; scores less than 0.60 reflect lower levels of marketing practice (Brodie, Coviello, Brookes and Little, 1997; Coviello, Brodie, Brookes and Palmer, 2003). It can be noticed that both countries follow similar patterns.

Market Served

The data was also analysed with respect to the market served. Respondents were asked to classify their customers as either consumers or business to business, and their products as either goods or services. This data has been crossed tabulated by country and marketing typology as illustrated in Table 4. The figures in bold reflect where the weight of respondents' firms lie and hence show that, though there are some differences due to the sample structure, the data indicates a trend whereby B2C tends to be transactional in marketing practice, whilst B2B is relational and pluralistic.

Market Orientation

Table 5 shows the results of the cross tabulation between scores for each element of market orientation together with the overall score, by

TABLE 4. Marketing Typology by Country and Product/Market–% Respondents

	Consumer Goods		Consumer Services		B2B Goods		B2B Services	
	Arg	UK	Arg	UK	Arg	UK	Arg	UK
Transactional	N = 7	N = 0	N = 6	N = 4	N = 1	N = 1	N = 14	N = 2
	63.6		**50**	**40**	5.3	10	26.4	6.7
Relational	N = 4	N = 1	N = 1	N = 3	N = 6	N = 5	N = 11	N = 7
	36.4	50	8.3	30	**54.5**	**50**	**57.9**	23.3
Pluralistic	N = 0	N = 1	N = 5	N = 3	N = 5	N = 4	N = 7	N = 21
		50	41.7	30	**45.5**	**40**	**36.8**	**70**

TABLE 5. Market Orientation

	Transactional		Relational		Pluralistic	
Orientation criteria	Arg (N = 14)	UK (N = 7)	Arg (N = 19)	UK (N = 17)	Arg (N = 22)	UK (N = 31)
Generation	19.2	18.3	20.0	18.0	20.6	19.4
Dissemination	11.2	14.0	15.4	13.5	15.5	15.7
Responsiveness	27.3	27.0	27.0	26.0	31.0	26.5
Overall Marketing Orientation	57.4	59.3	62.5	57.6	67.1	61.6

country and the marketing typology. The MARKOR instrument measures the extent to which each of three elements contribute to the overall measure of marketing orientation. These elements relate to the generation of intelligence relating to current and future customer needs, the dissemination of that intelligence across departments and the degree to which the organization responds as a consequence. The scores represent the extent to which the behaviours are expressed along each of the three dimensions measured by the MARKOR instrument (Kohli, Jaworski and Kumar, 1993). The higher the score, the greater the extent to which the characteristic is demonstrated. There were no statistical differences between each element of the data.

Marketing Outcomes

In order to assess marketing outcomes respondents were offered a range of comparative and relative criteria in order that they could indicate the importance of the criterion to the firm and performance as assessed by it. The criteria offered included sales growth, new customer gain, customer retention, profitability, customer satisfaction and achievement of market share (Table 6).

The only criterion that was consistently used by all respondents was relative sales growth. Return on investment (ROI) in comparison to competitors is also included as a measure of corporate performance. The table therefore records relative sales growth, as a measure of marketing outcome (MOt), and comparative ROI. The table records these by country and typology, and also indicates the frequency of usage of the criterion. Performance outcome was assessed by respondents on a 1-5 scale, where 1 = much worse and 5 = much better. As with other CMP research projects commonly used measure of sales growth were adopted, as this is normally regarded as indicative of the firm's effectiveness in the market (Walker and Ruekert, 1987), and is considered relatively easy information for managers to provide (Coviello et al., 2002).

DISCUSSION

Theoretical proposition 1: *Firms in developed markets adopt relational marketing practices in comparison to firms in turbulent markets.*

Table 3 demonstrates how the five typologies of marketing practice identified by the CMP group can be clustered into transactional, rela-

TABLE 6. Marketing Outcomes (MOt) and Corporate Performance (CP) Mean Scores (1-5 Scale)

		Argentina		UK	
Marketing Typology		MOt (Sales Growth)	CP (Comp ROI)	MOt (Sales Growth)	CP (Comp ROI)
Transactional	Outcome	3.15	3.44	3.71	3.00
	Usage	*4.79*		*4.00*	
Relational	Outcome	2.67	3.08	2.56	3.01
	Usage	*4.37*		*3.82*	
Pluralistic	Outcome	3.23	2.73	3.12	3.10
	Usage	*4.55*		*4.08*	

tional and pluralistic categories. The data demonstrates a good fit between the typologies and the clusters identified. It also shows a very high degree of consistency between the Argentine and UK data. When these clusters are then tested against the data for market orientation, Table 3, this again shows a high degree of consistency both between the clusters and data from the two countries.

This would strongly suggest that there is little difference between the UK and Argentina in terms of market orientation or marketing practice. This would suggest that the influence of market turbulence is low. This does not confirm the first proposition.

Theoretical proposition 2: *That marketing practice will vary by the profile of the market served.*

Previous work by members of the CMP group demonstrates that marketing practice varies with respect to the type of market served (Coviello, Brodie, Brookes and Palmer, 2003). The data in Table 4 is indicative but insufficiently rigorous for strong positive support to be ascribed to this theoretical proposition. However the direction indicated by the data is very consistent with the previous findings. Consumer goods and services are more strongly associated with transactional marketing practice, whilst the business-to-business area is the domain of relational and pluralistic marketing practices. The previous work of the CMP group was an international study comparing data from the UK and New Zealand, both developed economies. The additional comparative data from Argentina would once again suggest that the moderating effect of market turbulence on marketing practice is low.

Theoretical proposition 3: *That a higher degree of market orientation will be associated with relational marketing practice.*

There is some evidence to support this theoretical proposition particularly with respect to Argentina and when looking at the overall market orientation (Table 5). This demonstrates an increasing level of market orientation as marketing practice develops from transactional to relational and finally pluralistic. This tendency cannot be seen with UK data. It was previously suggested that in the much more stable UK general and market environment that a more relational level of marketing practice would give differentiation and competitive advantage. This initial suggestion is not supported by the findings, but leads to the further suggestion that high market turbulence can influence market orientation, which would suggest a fruitful opportunity for further research.

Theoretical proposition 4: *That different marketing typologies will be associated with different measures of marketing outcomes.*

The instrument gathered data on the use of a range of business performance and marketing outcome measures. Analysis of the data demonstrated that sales growth and profitability were the only consistent measures reported by respondents. There was no suggestion that firms practising relational or pluralistic styles of marketing used alternative measures such as customer retention or customer profitability.

This may be because of the difficulties associated with obtaining reliable data on these measures or that the instrument and sample sizes were inappropriate. We propose that more inductive work, such as detailed case study work with leading exponents of relationship marketing, will give a firmer basis on which to identify constructs appropriate to analyse and measure marketing outcomes relevant to relationship practice.

Theoretical proposition 5A: *That firm performance is not associated with the typology of marketing practice.*

Theoretical proposition 5B: *That marketing outcomes are associated with the typology of marketing practice.*

Theoretical proposition 5C: *That relational and pluralistic marketing practices will deliver higher levels of marketing outcomes.*

These theoretical propositions capture the view that corporate performance is influenced by many variables, including marketing practice. This is therefore too coarse a measure about which to draw conclusions concerning the influence of marketing practice. We, therefore, introduced the marketing outcomes construct in order to more directly relate marketing practice with results. We further suggested that a more relational level of marketing practice would deliver higher levels of marketing outcome, but that this would not necessarily be reflected in corporate performance due to the influence of the many other variables.

Table 6 shows that for the UK, a developed economy, the comparative ROI figures, as a measure of corporate performance, are very similar. This would support theoretical propositions 5A and 5B, as the figures for sales growth, a measure of marketing outcome, do vary with respect to the marketing typology. The transactional cluster in particular, for both Argentina and the UK, shows high levels of sales growth. These findings would not support theoretical proposition 5C. Interestingly this does suggest that the marketing outcome varies by marketing practice but not in the direction anticipated. However we must exercise caution as different marketing practices may prove to have other measures of marketing outcomes that may demonstrate benefit. For example relational practice could perhaps be judged by measures of customer or account profitability or customer retention, measures that may be more consistent with the marketing practice.

The results with respect to Argentina are much less clear-cut which raises interesting questions as to whether the differences noted are due to the type of economy, the measures used, or the research methodology itself. It will be of considerable interest to replicate this work and to include other developed and transitional economies.

However, the measures of marketing outcome, the instrument and sample size all need further refinement in order to obtain better indicative data. With the current levels of interest being shown in business and marketing performance we believe that this is an area worthy of further investigation. It is important to note that we do not seek proof of causality between these variables, but seek to generate insight and understanding in order to develop the theoretical model further.

CONCLUSIONS AND FUTURE RESEARCH

This is an exploratory study that seeks to respond to the original question posed by Kohli, Jaworski and Kumar on the generalisability of the positive effects of market orientation on performance in developing economies. The limitations imposed on the work by the constraints on sample size and representation in certain categories has been noted. It is proposed that within the epistemological framework of the study the test of our findings is one of explanation and understanding rather than an alternative test of proof. Whilst the quantitative data has limitations, the theoretical propositions and findings provide a sound basis for confirmatory work in this novel and previously unresearched area.

The authors based their work on a research framework developed by Matsuno and Mentzer, but use a radically different methodology. Matsuno and Mentzer used strategy as a modifier of the Kohli and Jaworski market orientation-corporate performance relationship. This paper suggests two modifications to the Matsuno and Mentzer model, first, to substitute strategy with the contemporary marketing practice typologies as a modifier. Secondly, to use marketing outcomes as an alternative to corporate performance. Finally, in order to address the generalisability of the model in developing economies, the study was conducted in both a developed economy (the UK) and an emerging economy (Argentina).

To guide theory development, a theoretical model and theoretical propositions have been developed. These have been tested against the data. The methodology and philosophical position are consistent with the unique and revelatory nature of the study. As a result of this work, we do not seek to provide proof of the relationship between variables or to demonstrate causality. Rather, we seek to build and develop understanding of the mechanisms at work and to provide further insights as the basis for further work. In the discussion we have been able to demonstrate strong support for some theoretical propositions, but with others this study allows the opportunity for further research.

The input side of the model demonstrates reasonable and credible consistency. Overall, the result suggests that market turbulence has little influence on market orientation and marketing practice. However, contrary to our original suppositions that marketing practice will be more relational in a developed economy, our results would suggest that the opposite is true. This is further supported by the most recent findings using the CMP framework (Wagner, 2004), which shows that Russian firms are more relational than transactional in terms of their marketing practice. This is an intriguing result in itself, but demonstrates the value of using the CMP framework in order to give greater insight and understanding.

The results also support previous findings from the CMP group in that marketing practice varies with respect to the product/market relationship. Consumer markets tend to be transactionally orientated, whilst in business-to-business markets, relational and pluralistic practice is more evident.

Concerning the outcomes of marketing practice, the results are much less clear. Though the CMP framework has proved valuable in this study, measures of marketing outcomes and corporate performance need further refinement for useful conclusions to be drawn. However, there is some support for the argument proposed that whilst corporate performance can be composed of multiple variables that act to average out the influence of marketing practice, marketing outcomes can and do vary with respect to the type of marketing that is practised. In particular, we would be interested to investigate further whether different measures of performance are used depending on the type of marketing practice.

The study has contributed in a number of important areas, in particular, in the direct comparisons of a transitional and developed economy. The study has a number of limitations in that it is bounded by the context in which it has been conducted. In addition, the sample size is limited, particularly for more detailed statistical analysis. It is also proposed that further refinement of the instrument, particularly with respect to business performance data, is required. We also propose that there is an opportunity for further qualitative work as a pre-cursor to more conceptual development and empirical fieldwork.

NOTES

1. The Contemporary Marketing Practice group is an international group of researchers who have the twin objectives of profiling marketing practices in an international context and developing insight and understanding of how firms relate to their markets. Further details can be found at http://cmp.auckland.ac.nz

2. The CMP group is an international research team investigating aspects of marketing practice. It has developed a classification scheme to describe current marketing practices (see Coviello et al., 1997 and 2002) and has published extensively on the empirical evidence and the conceptual framework.

REFERENCES

Berry, L.L. (1983), Relationship Marketing of Services: Growing Interest, Emerging Perspectives, *Journal of the Academy of Marketing Science, Vol 23, No 4*, pp. 236-245.

Bhuian, S.N. (1998), An Empirical Examination of Market Orientation in Saudi Arabian Manufacturing Companies, *Journal of Business Research, Vol 43, No 1*, 13-25.

Bititci, U.S. (1994), Measuring Your Way to Profit, *International Journal of Management Decision, Vol 32, No 6*, 16-24.

Blaikie, N. (1993), *Approaches To Social Enquiry*, Oxford: Blackwell.

Bollen, K.A. (1989), *Structural Equations with Latent Variables*, New York: John Wiley and Sons.

Brady, J., Davis, I. (1993), Marketing's Mid-Life Crisis, *McKinsey Quarterly*.

Brodie, R.J., Coviello, N.E., Brookes, R.W., Little, V. (1997), Towards a Paradigm Shift in Marketing? An Examination of Current Marketing Practices, *Journal of Marketing Management, Vol 13, No 5*, 383-406.

Christopher, M., Payne, A., Ballantyne, D. (1991), *Relationship Marketing*, Oxford: Butterworth-Heinemann.

Coviello, N., Brodie, R., Brookes, R., Palmer, R. (2003), Assessing the Role of e-Marketing in Contemporary Marketing Practice, *Journal of Marketing Management*, 19(7), 857-881.

Coviello, Brodie, Danaher and Johnston (2002), How Firms Relate to their Markets: An Empirical Examination of Contemporary Marketing Practices, *Journal of Marketing, Vol 66, No 2*.

Coviello, N.E., R. Milley and B. Marcolin (2001), Understanding IT-enabled Interactivity in Contemporary Marketing, *Journal of Interactive Marketing*, 15(4), 18-33.

Dawes, J. (2000), Market Orientation and Company Profitability: Further Empirical Evidence Incorporating Longitudinal Data, *Australian Journal of Management, forthcoming*.

Day, G, Montgomery, D (1999), Charting New Directions for Marketing, *Journal of Marketing, Vol 63*, 3-13.

Dess, G.G., Robinson, R.B. (1984), Measuring Organisational Performance in the Absence of Objective Measures: The Case of the Privately Held Firm and Conglomerate Business Unit, *Strategic Management Journal, Vol 5*, 265-263.

Easton, G. (1995), Case Research as a Methodology for Industrial Networks: A Realist Apologia, Proc of IMP 11th International Conference, Manchester.

Gatignon, H., Xuereb, J. (1997), Measuring Performance of International Joint Ventures. *Journal of International Business Studies,Vol 22, No 2*, 249-63.

Geringer, J.M. & L. Herbert (1991), Measuring Performance of International Joint Ventures, *Journal of International Business Studies, Vol 22, No 12*, 249-263.

Golden, P.A., Doney, P.M., Johnson, D.M., Smith, J.R. (1995), The Dynamics of a Marketing Orientation in Transition Economies: A Study of Russian Firms, *Journal of International Marketing, Vol 3, No 2*, 29-49.

Greenley, G.E. (1995), Market Orientation and Company Performance: Empirical Evidence from UK Companies, *British Journal of Management, Vol 6*, 1-13.

Grönroos, C. (1990), The Marketing Strategy Continuum: Towards a Marketing Concept for the 1990s. *Swedish School of Economics and Business Administration Working Papers*, 201.

Grönroos, C. (1992), Facing the Challenges of Service Competition: The Economies of Service, in Knst, P. and Lemmik, J. (Eds), *Quality Management in Services*, Assen/Maastricht: Van Gorcum.

Gummesson, E. (2000), *Total Relationship Marketing*, Oxford, Butterworth and Heinemann.

Gummesson, E., Lehtinen, U., Grönroos, C. (1997), Comment on Nordic Perspectives of Relationship Marketing, *European Journal of Marketing, Vol 31, No 1*, 10.

Hair, J.F., Andersen, R.E., Tatham, R.L., Black, W.C. (1998), *Multivariate Data Analysis*. Prentice Hall: New Jersey, USA.

Hakansson, H., Snehota, I. (1995), *Developing Relationships in Business Networks*, London, Routledge.

Hakansson, H. (Ed) (1982), *International Marketing and Purchasing of Industrial Goods*, New York: Wiley.

Hartenian, L.S., Gudmundson, D.E. (2000), Cultural Diversity in Small Business:

Hirschman, E.C. (1986), Humanistic Enquiry in Marketing Research: Philosophy, Method and Criteria, *Journal of Marketing Research, Vol 23*, Aug, 237-249.

Holmlund, M. (1997), *Perceived Quality in Business Relationships*, Helsinki: Swedish School of Economic and Business Administration.

Homburg, C., Pflesser, C. (2000), A Multiple-Layer Model of Market-Oriented Organisational Culture: Measurement Issues and Performance Outcomes, *Journal of Marketing Research, Vol 27*, 449-462.

Implications for Firm Performance, *Journal of Developmental Entrepreneurship*,

Jaworski, B.J., Kohli, A.K. (1993), Market Orientation: Antecedents and Consequences, *Journal of Marketing, Vol 57*, July, 53-70.

Kohli, A.K., Jaworski, B.J. (1990), Market Orientation: The Construct, Research Propositions, and Managerial Implications, *Journal of Marketing, Vol 54*, April, 1-18.

Kohli, A.K., Jaworski, B.J., Kumar, A. (1993), MARKOR: A Measure of Market Orientation, *Journal of Marketing Research, Vol 30*, November, 467-477.

Martin, J.H., Martin, B.A., Grbac, B. (1998), Employee Involvement and Market Orientation in a Transition Economy: Importance, Problems and a Solution, *Journal of Managerial Issues, Vol 10, No 4*, 485-497.

Matsuno and Mentzer (2000), The Effects of Strategy Type on The Market Orientation-Performance Relationship, *Journal of Marketing, Vol 64, No 4*, 1-16.

Mavondo, F.T., Farrell, M.A. (2000), Measuring Market Orientation: Are There Differences Between Business Marketers and Consumer Marketers?, *Australian Journal of Management, Vol 25, No 2*, 223-224.

Menon, A., Bharadaj, S., Adidam, P.T. and Edison, S. (1999), Antecedents and Consequences of Marketing Strategy Making: A Model and A Test, *Journal of Marketing*, 62, April, 19-41.

Miles, R.E., Snow, C.C. (1978), *Organisational Strategy Structure, and Process*, New York: McGraw-Hill.

Miller, D. (1987), The Structural and Environmental Correlates of Business Strategy, *Strategic Management Journal, Vol 8, No 1*, 55-76.

Mintzberg, H. (1994), *The Rise and Fall of Strategic Planning*, Hemel Hempstead: Prentice Hall.

Morgan, R.M., Hunt, S.D. (1994), The Commitment-Trust Theory of Relationship Marketing, *Journal of Marketing, Vol 58*, July, 20-38.

Narver, J.C., Slater, S.F. (1990), The Effect of a Market Orientation on Business Profitability, *Journal of Marketing, Vol 54*, October, 20-35.

Neelankavil, J.P., Mathur, A., and Zhang, Y. (2000), Determinants of Managerial Performance: A Cross-Cultural Comparison of the Perceptions of Middle-Level Managers in Four Countries, *Journal of International Business Studies*, 31(1), 121-40.

Olsen, H.W. (2001), Market Orientation: Towards an Understanding in Developing Marketplaces of South America, PhD Dissertation, Old Dominion University.

Pelham, A.M. (1997), Market Orientation and Performance: The Moderating Effects of Product and Customer Differentiation, *Journal of Business and Industrial Marketing, Vol 12, No 5*, 276-296.

Pels, J. (1999), Exchange Relationships in Consumer Markets? *European Journal of Marketing, Vol 33, No 1/2*, 19-37.

Pitt, L., Caruana, A., Berthon, P.R. (1996), Market Orientation and Business Performance: Some European Evidence, *International Marketing Review, Vol 13, No 1*, 5-18.

Selnes, F., Jaworski, B.J., Kohli, A.K. (1996), Market Orientation in US and Scandinavian Companies, *Scandinavian Journal of Management, Vol 12, No 2*, 139-157.

Sigauw, J.A., Diamantopoulos, A. (1995), Measuring Market Orientation: Some Evidence on Narver and Slater's Three Component Scale, *Journal of Strategic Marketing, Vol 3*, 77-88.

Sheth, J.N., Gardner, D.M., Garrett, D.E. (1988), *Marketing Theory, Evolution and Evaluation*, New York: Wiley.

Sheth, J.N., Parvatiyar, A. (1995), *The Evolution of Relationship Marketing, International Business Review, Vol 4, No 4*, 397-418.

Styles, C. (1998), Performance Measures in Australia and the United Kingdom, *Journal of International Marketing, Vol 6, No 3*.

Uncles, M. (2000), Market Orientation, *Australian Journal of Management, Vol 25, No 2*, i-ix.

Venkataraman, N., Ramanajam, V. (1986), Measurements of business performance in strategic research: A comparison of approaches, *Academic of Management Review, Vol 11, No 4*, 801-814.

Walker, O.C., Ruekert, R.W. (1987), Marketing's Role in the Implementation of Business Strategies: A Critical Review and Conceptual Framework, *Journal of Marketing, Vol 51*, July, 15-33.

Wagner, R. (2004), Contemporary Marketing Practices in Russia, *in review*.

Webster, F.E., Jr. (1992), The Changing Role of Marketing in the Corporation, *Journal of Marketing*, 56 (October), 1-17.

Five Aspects of Marketing Classified by Exchange and Managerial Dimensions

	Transaction Marketing	Database Marketing	e-Marketing	Interaction Marketing	Network Marketing
Purpose of Exchange	Economic transaction	Information and economic transaction	Information-generating dialogue between a seller and many identified buyers	Interpersonal relationships between a buyer and seller	Connected relationships between firms
Nature of Communication	Firm "to" mass market	Firm "to" targeted segment or individuals	Firm using technology to communicate "with" and "among" many individuals (who may form groups)	Individuals "with" individuals (across organizations)	Firms "with" firms (involving individuals)
Type of Contact	Arms-length, impersonal	Personalized (yet distant)	Interactive (via technology)	Face-to-face, interpersonal (close, based on commitment, trust, and cooperation)	Impersonal–interpersonal (ranging from distant to close)
Duration of Exchange	Discrete (yet perhaps over time)	Discrete and over time (occasional yet personalized)	Continuous (but interactivity occurs in real-time)	Continuous (ongoing and mutually adaptive, short or long term)	Continuous (stable yet dynamic, may be short or long term)
Formality in Exchange	Formal	Formal (yet personalized via technology)	Formal (yet customized and/or personalized via interactive technology)	Formal and informal (i.e., at both a business and social level)	Formal and informal (i.e., at both a business and social level)
Managerial Intent	Customer attraction (to satisfy the customer at a profit)	Customer retention (to satisfy the customer, increase profit, and attain other objectives such as increased loyalty, decreased customer risk, etc.)	Creation of IT-enabled dialogue	Interaction (to establish, develop, and facilitate a cooperative relationship for mutual benefit)	Co-ordination (interaction between sellers, buyers, and other parties across multiple firms for mutual benefit, resource exchange, market access, etc.)
Managerial Focus	Product or brand	Product/brand and customers (in a targeted market)	Managing IT-enabled relationships between the firm and many individuals	Relationships between individuals	Connected relationships between firms (in a network)
Managerial Investment	Internal marketing assets (focusing on product/service, price, distribution, promotion capabilities)	Internal marketing assets (emphasizing information and database technology capabilities)	Internal operational assets (IT, website, logistics) Functional systems integration	External market assets (focusing on establishing and developing a relationship with another individual)	External market assets (focusing on developing the firm's position in a network of firms)
Managerial Level	Functional marketers (e.g., Sales Manager, Product Manager)	Specialist marketers (e.g., Customer Service Manager, Loyalty Manager)	Marketing specialists (with technology specialists) Senior managers	Employees and managers (from across functions and levels in the firm)	Senior managers

Source: Adapted from Coviello et al., 1997, 2000; Coviello, Brodie, Brookes, and Palmer, 2003.

The Role of Domestic Animosity in Consumer Choice: Empirical Evidence from Germany

Wolfgang Hinck

SUMMARY. The paper argues that specific choice and preference constructs previously only applied in international research may explain certain domestic phenomena better than those concepts typically used in domestic choice and preference studies. The animosity model of foreign product purchase is employed within the German consumer market. Results suggest that the previously uninvestigated notion of domestic animosity is responsible for a recent cross-segmental preference reversal in the eastern part of the nation. The outcome of the study has implications for internal trade in countries across the globe, as well as for scientific marketing research. *[Article copies available for a fee from The Haworth Document Delivery Service: 1-800-HAWORTH. E-mail address: <docdelivery@ haworthpress.com> Website: <http://www.HaworthPress.com> © 2004 by The Haworth Press, Inc. All rights reserved.]*

KEYWORDS. Domestic animosity, choice and preference, Germany, consumer behavior

Wolfgang Hinck is affiliated with the Department of Management and Marketing, College of Business Administration, Louisiana State University in Shreveport, One University Place, Shreveport, LA 71115 (E-mail: whinck@pilot.LSUS.edu).

[Haworth co-indexing entry note]: "The Role of Domestic Animosity in Consumer Choice: Empirical Evidence from Germany." Hinck, Wolfgang. Co-published simultaneously in *Journal of Euromarketing* (International Business Press, an imprint of The Haworth Press, Inc.) Vol. 14, No. 1/2, 2004, pp. 87-104; and: *Marketing Issues in Western Europe: Changes and Developments* (eds: Erdener Kaynak, and Frédéric Jallat) International Business Press, an imprint of The Haworth Press, Inc., 2004, pp. 87-104. Single or multiple copies of this article are available for a fee from The Haworth Document Delivery Service [1-800-HAWORTH, 9:00 a.m. - 5:00 p.m. (EST). E-mail address: docdelivery@haworthpress.com].

INTRODUCTION

A vast number of authors in consumer behavior and marketing psychology have studied the issue of why consumers choose or prefer one product to the other. For comparisons between domestic products (hereafter: domestic-domestic), recently outlined reasons for choices or preferences included price considerations (Olshavsky et al., 1995; Mazumdar and Papatla, 2000), perceived quality (Gross et al., 1993; Creyer and Ross, 1997), greater awareness or familiarity (Coupey et al., 1998; Macdonald and Sharp, 2000), perceived risk (Mitchell, 1999), social status demonstration (Marcoux et al., 1997), nostalgia (Holbrook, 1993), and high switching costs (Carpenter and Nakamoto, 1989), as well as several other well-established constructs relating to product attributes, perceived benefits, and consumer attitudes, beliefs and sensory preferences (see for examples, Currim and Schneider, 1991; Alba et al., 1992; Dabholkar, 1994; Januszewska and Viaene, 2001; King and Balasubramanian, 1994; Dhar, 1997; Nowlis and Simonson, 1997).

Additionally, in studies of situations where domestic products were chosen over foreign products (hereafter: domestic-foreign), some foreign-specific explanatory variables and constructs were observed, such as country-of-origin effects (see for examples, Chao, 1993; Kaynak et al., 2000; Ziamou et al., 1999), nationalism (Balabanis et al., 2001), ethnocentrism (see for examples, Sharma et al., 1995; Kaynak and Kara, 2001; Supphellen and Rittenburg, 2001; Watson and Wright, 2000), helping behavior (Olsen et al., 1993; Granzin and Olsen, 1998), animosity (Klein et al., 1998; Klein, 2002), and patriotism (Balabanis et al., 2001; Han, 1988). Whereas the domestic-domestic group has in common a very specific nature that will differ from one product to the other (although both products may come from the same country of origin), the domestic-foreign group has in common that all constructs but one lead to a preference for all domestic products over all foreign products (independent from specific countries of origin). The only exception is the animosity model of foreign product purchase (Klein et al., 1998), suggesting that only one specific country–but all of the products from that country–could be affected.

While most–if not all–of the domestic-domestic constructs have also been applied in studies that focused on preference and choice processes in domestic-foreign situations, no study could be found that used the opposite approach, that is, attempting to explain domestic-domestic choice processes with a construct originally generated from the research in domestic-foreign situations. It is intuitively, logically, and empirically reasonable to argue that as long as domestic-domestic variables are sufficient to explain phenomena in domestic choice situations, the use of other constructs is unnecessary. However, this paper will argue that the application of selected foreign-domestic constructs may provide a better explanation for phenomena in specific domestic-domestic situations. The paper will coin the term "domestic animosity," a term describing near-hostile feelings among citizens of one nation. The example chosen to illustrate the argument is the case of Germany.

EXPLAINING THE NEUE LÄNDER SITUATION

After the historic fall of the Berlin Wall on November 9, 1989, manufacturers and distributors from the Federal Republic of Germany began entering the markets of the German Democratic Republic on a large scale (Händel, 1991; Müller, 1996; Schmoll, 1996; Lay, 1997). At the point in time of German reunification on October 3, 1990, companies from the Western states (*Alte Bundesländer, or: Alte Länder*) already possessed a market share of over 75 percent of all products sold in the five new states (*Neue Bundesländer, or: Neue Länder*) (Cote, 1990b). When Neue Länder consumers continued to express their desire for Western goods and practically ignored items from the East (King et al., 1996; Kersting, 1997; Müller, 1997), basically all locally produced goods disappeared from the shelves in Eastern Germany and were replaced with Western production (Grunert et al., 1995).

However, over the past several years, Eastern German consumers increasingly disregarded Alte Länder products and started preferring products manufactured by companies located in the new states (see for examples, La Roche, 1996; Müller, 1996; Rohnstock, 1996; Lay, 1997; Müller, 1997). These locally produced items included, among several other products, food (brands such as *Bautzener, Halberstädter, Spreewald*), tobacco (*Juno, Cabinet, Karo*), soft drinks (*Club, Vita*), alcoholic beverages (*Rotkäppchen, Hasseröder, Nordhäuser*), laundry detergents (*Fit, Spee*), cosmetics (*Florena*), bicycles (*Diamant*), refrigerators (*Foron*), tires (*Pneumant*), watches (*Glashütte, Zeiss-Jena*), porcelain (*Meißner*), magazines (*Eulenspiegel, Guter Rat*), and TV programs (*ORB, MDR*) (see for examples, Economist, 2002; Posny, 1995; Martell, 1996; Rohnstock, 1996; Schmoll, 1996; Lay, 1997; Müller, 1997; Willnecker, 1997). Within a short period of time, Eastern products regained market shares of up to 50 percent (Lunze, 1996). Over the past few years, this development continued and led to market shares of over 50 percent for specific Eastern products in segments that had previously been controlled by Alte Länder companies (Waldmann, 1999; Huster, 2000).

No literature can be found that empirically investigates this particular phenomenon of preference reversal. Possible explanations from previous research on choice and preference may not be valid. One of the major problems involved is the lack of applicability of many of the domestic-domestic constructs on a general, cross-segmental consumer preference change, as in the case of the situation in the German consumer market. Previous research has focused on specific products or product groups, rather than on preferences throughout different segments or markets. For example, lower price could possibly explain Eastern Germans' preference for East tobacco over Alte Länder tobacco, but could possibly not explain the preference for East watches and porcelain which are of significantly higher price than their Western counterparts. The choice of the latter could be explained by higher quality or social status demonstration, but this construct could not be applied to the preference for Neue Länder alcoholic beverages or soft drinks, since their quality is perceived to be lower. Similarly, the constructs of greater familiarity, less perceived risk, or nostalgia could possibly explain the preference for Eastern laundry detergents and food, but would possibly fail to sufficiently address products such as TV programs (new programs may not provide greater familiarity), refrigerators (Eastern brands' low quality may present higher perceived risk), or soft drinks (new brands may not satisfy nostalgia) (see for examples, La Roche, 1996; Lunze, 1996; Martell, 1996; Rohnstock, 1996; Schmoll, 1996; Lay, 1997; Müller, 1997; Willnecker, 1997; Emcke, 1999). Therefore, unless it is argued that a large number of single small-scale phenomena are occurring simultaneously, rather than only one single large-scale phenomenon, constructs from previous domestic-domestic research on choice and preference cannot explain the events.

From the viewpoint of the phenomenon being single large-scale, the stated domestic-foreign constructs appear to be better suited for explanation, since they accommodate cross-segmental and cross-market consumer behavior. With the exception of the animosity concept, however, these constructs imply a general preference for Neue Länder products over all foreign products. That does not appear to be the case. For example, there is no indication that domestic companies from the Alte Länder producing in the Neue Länder are preferred over foreign (non-German) companies producing there (Waldmann, 1999). Many of the companies successfully serving the Eastern German markets are, in fact, foreign companies producing in the Neue Länder (Lunze, 1996; Martell, 1996; Willnecker, 1997). Consequently, among the domestic-foreign constructs, only the animosity model of foreign product purchase with its idea of specific negative attitudes towards a source country and its consequent rejection of the source country's products appears to be applicable to the situation under consideration. Although Klein et al.'s (1998) study explicitly addressed international markets, the model could technically be extended to domestic animosity and as such applied to the situation in the Neue Länder. The issue is now if–besides technical applicability–there is also sufficient theoretical reason for assuming that domestic animosity can explain the shift in the Neue Länder markets.

ANIMOSITY IN THE NEUE LÄNDER

Face validity for the use of the animosity construct is easily established. Klein et al. (1998) define animosity "as the remnants of antipathy related to previous or ongoing military, political, or economic events [that] will affect consumers' purchase behavior in the international market-place" (p. 90). The authors further state that animosity may have many sources, ranging "from a relatively benign rivalry as a result of sharing a contiguous border (e.g., the United States and Canada) to more serious manifestations stemming from previous military events or recent economic or diplomatic disputes" (p. 90). Based on this assumption, possible sources for animosity of Neue Länder citizen can be identified easily.

Soon after the Berlin wall fell, Eastern Germans already considered the events to be painful experiences (Cote, 1990b; Economist, 2000), and perceived that they were being treated "like second-class citizens in their own country" (Cote, 1990a: p. 36). Preferential treatment in restaurant and shopping malls was given to Western German customers who possessed larger amounts of hard currency. Although the currency availability problem was ultimately solved with the reunification, Eastern Germans soon experienced several other difficulties. First of all, the "new" Germany was basically the "old" Federal Republic, only extended to the East (Siebert, 1991; Schröter and Röber, 1997; Parnell, 1999). Eastern considerations were ignored during the planning stages of the reunification, and while the everyday routines of the Alte Länder citizens remained unchanged by the unification, almost all aspects of life radically changed for citizens in the East, with arrangements often worsening their situation (Büchtemann and Schupp, 1992; Sweeney and Hardaker, 1994; Nill, 2001).

Additional problems were created through the activities of the *Treuhandanstalt*, a governmental agency that was responsible to help turning Eastern state-owned firms into private organizations (Clarke-Hill and Robinson, 1996; Hau, 1998). Their activities, often character-ized by scandals and bribery incidents (leading to the assassination of the agency's president by leftwing terrorists), led to a significant in-crease of unemployment in the Neue Länder (Sweeney and Hardaker, 1994; Grunert et al., 1995). In total, eighty percent of all industrial jobs in the Neue Länder were lost following the activities of the *Treuhan-danstalt* (Müller, 1996), while–at the same time–the Western German economy expanded significantly (Büchtemann and Schupp, 1992; Grunert et al., 1995). A major problem in this regard was that Alte Länder and foreign investors often misused governmental financial incentives. Rather than improving Eastern production facilities to create new jobs, the facilities were sold in pieces, thus destroying all existing and poten-tial jobs. Consequently, the unemployment rate in the Neue Länder grew up to twice as high as in the West (Ewing, 1999). Those Eastern Germans who remained in their positions earned significantly less than their counterparts in the Alte Länder (Sweeney and Hardaker, 1994).

Further problems were created by Western German politicians and business people who made various promises without keeping them (Nash, 1995; Lay, 1997); by Western German managers pressing their business cultures onto Neue Länder firms (Randlesome, 2000); by Alte Länder wholesalers and retailers who rejected to distribute goods from Eastern German production (Nash, 1995; Lunze, 1996; Zimmermann, 1998); and by Alte Länder consumers who only reluctantly or not at all bought those few products from the East that had made it into Alte Länder stores (Schmoll, 1996; Kersting, 1997). Differences in opinions (Banaszak, 1998), beliefs (Wydmusch, 2000), attitudes (Adler and Brayfield, 1996; Kirkcaldy et al., 1999), values (Borg and Braun, 1996), and cultural dimensions (Weber, 1991; Sweeney and Hardaker, 1994; Grunert et al., 1995; Howard, 1995; Emcke, 1999) established more po-tential sources for tensions, as did the frequent usage of the negative ep-ithets "Ossie" (for Germans from the Neue Länder) and "Wessie" (for Germans from the Alte Länder), which are used by Eastern and Western Germans when referring to the other group, respectively (Stern, 1991; Emcke, 1999).

In summary, it can be convincingly proposed that the outlined prob-lems established a feeling of animosity of Eastern Germans towards

Western Germany, particularly considering the fact that over 50 percent of Neue Länder citizen state that they were happier with their former system (Lynch, 1999). Based on the findings by Klein et al. (1998) indicating a causal relationship between animosity and product rejection independently of favorable product judgments, it can now be hypothesized that the situation in the Neue Länder could be in part explained by a rejection of products from the Western part of Germany, rather than simply by a pure preference for Eastern products.

To test the hypothesis of an effect of domestic animosity on purchasing willingness, Klein et al.'s (1998) questionnaire was used. Several authors have replicated the original animosity study since its original publication and confirmed the validity of the scales (see for examples, Klein, 2002; Nijssen et al., 1999; Hinck and Felix, 2000; Witkowski, 2000). In accordance with the foreign animosity model containing the four constructs animosity, willingness to purchase, product judgment, and ethnocentrism, the following two basic hypotheses were tested.

H_1: Domestic Animosity will emerge as a separate and distinct construct in the model.

H_2: Domestic Animosity will have a direct, negative impact on willingness to buy Alte Länder products independently of product judgments and ethnocentrism.

ANALYSES AND RESULTS

The questionnaire developed by Klein et al. (1998) contains 27 statements within the four constructs of product judgments, willingness to buy, consumer ethnocentrism, and animosity. The latter construct included the two sub-constructs of war animosity and economic animosity. Because of the specific situation, all three questions referring to war animosity were taken off the questionnaire, so that solely economic animosity was measured. The questionnaire was translated into German subsequently back-translated into English. Minor adjustments were made. Additionally, two changes were made as a result of a pretest. First of all, one question was deleted from the questionnaire because of its strong emic characteristics. Second, it was decided that the questionnaire administered in the Neue Länder would employ a 5-point Likert scale instead of the original 7-point scale (indicating agreement from "strongly agree" to "strongly disagree"). The reason for the reduction by two points was rather practical and based on the total number of questions. Since the questionnaire also contained 29 questions referring to two other studies, it was perceived that respondents would be more likely to answer all of the questions if their choices were more limited.

Data were then collected from adult consumers in the Neue Länder, and re-collected twelve months later. A separate analysis of the two datasets revealed no differences between the periods. In sampling, several important aspects were considered. Previous articles on consumer behavior and attitudes in Eastern and Western Germany have shown that responses may especially differ depending on the dimensions of gender (Scherhorn et al., 1990), age (GfK, 1997), proximity to former border (Feick and Gierl, 1996; Schmoll, 1996), North-South distribution (Usunier, 1991), rural-urban distribution (Schopphoven, 1991), and professional achievement (Büchtemann and Schupp, 1992). Therefore, an approach similar to mall intercept was chosen and the survey was conducted in four different locations, assuring North-Center-South discrimination, as well as rural-urban discrimination and border-proximity distribution. More specifically, questionnaires were administered in Bestensee (State of Brandenburg), Dohna (State of Saxony), Dresden (State of Saxony), and Stralsund (State of Mecklenburg-Vorpommern). Dresden and Stralsund are cities in the Southeast and North of the Neue Länder, respectively. Bestensee is a village approximately 20 miles south of West Berlin, and is located in the center of the Neue Länder. Dohna is a town, located approximately 15 miles east of Dresden. Additionally, diversity with regard to the dimensions of gender, age, profession, and professional achievement was taken into consideration.

With the support of local non-student citizens at each of the four locations, a total of 325 individuals were approached until all of the 200 planned questionnaires had been distributed. Stamped self-addressed envelopes were attached. A total of 146 questionnaires were returned, establishing a response rate of 45 percent of all individuals contacted, and 73 percent of total questionnaires distributed. All respondents were Germans who had lived in the Neue Länder for the past ten years and who, with the exception of one respondent, have grown up in the East. Sample characteristics are included in Table 1.

Descriptive statistics can be found in Table 2. As outlined before, a 5-point Likert scale was used. Higher ratings reflect greater willingness to buy, higher levels of consumer ethnocentrism, greater levels of do-

TABLE 1. Sample Characteristics (n = 146)

Gender	Male = 62 (42.5%) Female = 84 (57.5%)
Age	≤ 30 = 32 (21.9%) 31-40 = 47 (32.2%) 41-50 = 41 (28.1%) 51-60 = 17 (11.6%) > 60 = 9 (6.2%)
Location	City = 65 (44.5%) Town = 39 (26.7%) Rural = 42 (28.8%)
Job	Blue Collar = 27 (18.5%) Administrative = 51 (34.9%) Student = 12 (8.2%) Other = 56 (38.4%)
Annual Income (in DEM 1,000)	≤ 25 = 72 (49.3%) 25-50 = 63 (43.2%) 50-75 = 10 (6.8%) 75-100 = 0 (0%) > 100 = 1 (.7%)

TABLE 2. Descriptive Statistics

	Mean	Standard Deviation
Willingness to Buy	3.008	0.672
Consumer Ethnocentrism	2.831	0.877
Domestic Animosity	3.964	0.593
Product Judgment	4.109	0.561

mestic animosity towards Western Germany, and more positive product judgments.

The table shows that despite Neue Länder consumers' favorable judgments of the quality of Alte Länder products, they were indifferent with regard to their willingness to purchase those products. Domestic animosity appears to be strong, while consumer ethnocentrism seems to be surprisingly low, considering that the Neue Länder have repeatedly been the location of anti-foreign events.

In order to now test the existence of domestic animosity and its translation into rejection of Alte Länder products, two statistical techniques were used: principal component analysis and regression analysis. Principal component analysis was performed to confirm that the questionnaire items were related to the four constructs of economic animosity, consumer ethnocentrism, product judgment, and willingness to buy. The Bartlett test of sphericity indicated the appropriateness of the use of this statistical technique ($\chi^2 = 412$, p-value = .000). The sixteen statements reported in Table 3 were reduced to four constructs with four items representing each construct.

The results of the principal component analysis support Klein et al.'s (1998) measurement model. In particular, they confirm the emergence of economic animosity and consumer ethnocentrism as separate and distinct constructs and, thus, confirm H_1. In addition, Cronbach alpha statistics were greater than .6 and, hence, indicate that the constructs are reliable.

TABLE 3. The Constructs and Their Indicators

Constructs	Cronbach α
Willingness to Buy I would feel guilty if I bought a product from the Alte Länder. I would never buy a product from the Alte Länder. Whenever possible, I avoid buying a product from the Alte Länder. I do not like the idea of owning a product from the Alte Länder.	.7231
Consumer Ethnocentrism A good German does not buy foreign products. It is not right to purchase foreign products because it puts Germans out of jobs. We should purchase products manufactured in Germany instead of letting other countries get rich off us. We should buy from foreign countries only those products that we cannot obtain within our own country.	.8046
Domestic Animosity The Alte Länder want to gain power over the Neue Länder. The Alte Länder are taking advantage of the Neue Länder. The Alte Länder have too much influence in the Neue Länder. The Alte Länder are unfair with the Neue Länder.	.6627
Product Judgment Products made in the Alte Länder usually show a very clever use of color and design. Products made in the Alte Länder are very reliable. Products made in the Alte Länder are usually a good value for the money. Products made in the Alte Länder are carefully produced and have fine workmanship.	.7193

The next step involved estimating a regression model where the willingness to buy construct was set as the dependent variable and consumer ethnocentrism, product judgment, and economic animosity as the independent variables. Each construct was measured by a composite index of its underlying indicators, derived from (1) Klein et al.'s (1998) measurement model and (2) our principal component analysis. The sample was also split and regressed by age, gender, border proximity, location, profession, and income. Only the variables age and border proximity had discriminating character. Results are reported in Table 4.

The table shows that for obvious reasons, consumer ethnocentrism (a truly foreign-directed construct) does not affect the willingness to purchase products from the Alte Länder. More interestingly, the effect of *domestic* animosity on willingness to buy Western German products is even stronger than the effect of animosity in previous *cross*-national studies by Klein et al. (1998) and Witkowski (2000). This result confirms H_2 and suggests that animosity, in fact, is a construct that does not just explain international phenomena, but can also help explain domestic situations.

The results with regard to the variables age and border proximity were also interesting. Particularly with regard to age it is true that the older a respondent, the greater the effect of animosity on willingness to buy. This result does not confirm Klein et al.'s (1998) sub-group analysis that did not find significant differences between diverse age groups, but is consistent with a follow-up study that suggested that animosity increased with age (Klein and Ettenson, 1999). Based on the latter article and the findings of the present paper, it can be assumed that older consumers were more used to the systems and–as such–were hit harder by the changes. That could very easily explain a stronger negative affective

TABLE 4. Regression Coefficients (Willingness to Buy)

Variable	Total	Age ≤ 40	Age > 40	Closer to Border	Farther from Border
Domestic Animosity	−.37[b]	−.27[b]	−.41[b]	−.39[b]	−.28[b]
Product Judgment	.31[a]	.30[a]	.36[a]	.31[a]	.29[a]
Consumer Ethnocentrism	.041[c]	.039[c]	.046[c]	.025[c]	.008[c]

[a] = significant at p ≤ .01
[b] = significant at p ≤ .05
[c] = not significant
All coefficients are standardized.

response. Additionally, the present study finds that the closer a respondent resides to the former border, the stronger the effect of domestic animosity on willingness to purchase Alte Länder products.

DISCUSSION AND IMPLICATIONS

The purpose of the present study was to investigate the rejection of products from Western Germany by Eastern Germans, and to provide empirical evidence for the suggestion that part of the rejection of the products could be explained by a domestic animosity felt by Neue Länder towards the West. In addition, the study attempted to evaluate the extent to which constructs known from international research could be used to explain intranational phenomena. With these two objectives in mind, the results of the study have implications for both managerial action and scientific marketing research.

Most of all, the results provide a clearer understanding of a phenomenon that is taking place in Germany's Neue Länder. Strong negative, product-independent attitudes among consumers have become so significant that they directly affect the willingness to purchase products across categories and segments. It is particularly interesting that this situation is taking place within national boundaries. At a time where more and more research is targeting the globalization of markets, the investigation of domestic developments may have become increasingly neglected. At first, one might not expect that negative feelings within a specific country can become so powerful that they deter consumers from buying products of domestic origin. In addition, it could be argued that even if this is the case in Germany, it is probably a singular phenomenon of little importance to non-German companies. At second thought, however, the same experience could currently affect firms in almost every nation of the world. For example, although not previously studied, it is very well possible that the same phenomenon is taking place in Spain (where many Basques are quite critical towards the rest of the country), or in Great Britain (where the English, Scots, and Welsh may very possibly feel some domestic animosity beyond football). Many Eastern European countries and the United States appear to be even more prone to experience the effects of domestic animosity.

For marketing managers all over the globe, therefore, it is recommended to carefully investigate the chances of an occurrence of domestic animosity in their home markets. Specifically, German firms should adjust their marketing strategies to the situation in the market. The approaches employed could be similar to those frequently used to overcome country-of-origin effects (that is, de-emphasizing the product's origin). Special attention should be paid to the effects of age and former border proximity. As shown by the results, the purchasing behavior of younger respondents appears to be less affected by their feelings toward the West. A possible reason could be that these respondents were in their teens when Germany was united and, therefore, may be less used to–and less familiar with–the products from Eastern Germany. Additionally, they may in general exhibit a higher nationalistic affiliation with Germany as a whole than with Eastern Germany. The older generations, despite ten years of reunification at the time of data collection, may still harbor Eastern German nationalistic feelings and, thus, their feelings of animosity towards the Alte Länder would more strongly also affect their purchasing behavior, particularly since they are most likely still familiar with the former Neue Länder brands.

It is, furthermore, interesting that for those living closer to the former border, the effect of domestic animosity on purchasing behavior is much stronger than for those living further away from the border, although the degree of domestic animosity per se did not appear to significantly differ. A possible reason could be that although both share similar levels of animosity, those living closer to the border are more frequently exposed to–and reminded of–the circumstances that have led to the animosity in the first place. Therefore, it could be that a stronger intention to retaliate has developed. Once again, the implications for firms are to be sensitive about the possibility of domestic animosity and to respond accordingly. In order to regain market share, Alte Länder companies have to choose approaches different from those frequently chosen in the case of customer dissatisfaction or differentiation disadvantage. The present attempts of Western German practitioners may be destined for failure because of wrong underlying assumptions. With the results of this study at hand, firms may specifically address the issue of domestic animosity. Firms in other nations affected by the same phenomenon may proceed accordingly.

Besides its practical and managerial implications, this study also contributes to scientific marketing research. It is interesting to realize that constructs from cross-national research may be well suited for explanation of domestic occurrences. Nevertheless, it should be further investigated if the animosity construct, in fact, accurately reflects domestic animosity, as opposed to international animosity. The overall reliability measure for the domestic animosity construct ($\alpha = 0.6627$), although generally acceptable, is relatively small given the confirmatory nature of the principal component analysis. The relatively lower loadings on the animosity construct may also point towards the need for a slight modification of the statements.

Overall, more research is needed to investigate the occurrence and effect of domestic animosity. It is recommendable that authors in other nations replicate this study to gain a better picture of domestic animosity. Also, with additional research the animosity construct could be modified. Such modifications should yield better results in terms of construct reliability, variable and model significance, and generalizability.

REFERENCES

Adler, M.A. and Brayfield, A. (1996), "East-West differences in attitudes about employment and family in Germany," *The Sociological Quarterly*, Vol. 37, pp. 245-60.

Alba, J.W., Marmorstein, H. and Chattopadhyay, A. (1992), "Transitions in preference over time: the effects of memory on message persuasiveness," *Journal of Marketing Research*, Vol. 29, pp. 406-16.

Balabanis, G., Diamantopoulos, A., Mueller, R.D., and Melewar, T.C. (2001), "The impact of nationalism, patriotism and internationalism on consumer ethnocentric tendencies," *Journal of International Business Studies*, Vol. 32, pp. 157-75.

Banaszak, L.A. (1998), "East-West differences in German abortion," *Public Opinion Quarterly*, Vol. 62, pp. 545-82.

Borg, I. and Braun, M. (1996), "Work values in East and West Germany. different weights, but identical structures," *Journal of Organizational Behavior*, Vol. 17, pp. 541-55.

Büchtemann, C.F. and Schupp, J. (1992), "Repercussions of reunification: patterns and trends in the socio-economic transformation of East Germany," *Industrial Relations Journal*, Vol. 23, pp. 90-106.

Carpenter, G.S. and Nakamoto, K. (1989), "Consumer preference formation and pioneering advantage," *Journal of Marketing Research*, Vol. 26, pp. 285-98.

Chao, P. (1993), "Partitioning country of origin effects: consumer evaluations of a hybrid product," *Journal of International Business Studies*, Vol. 24, pp. 291-306.

Clarke-Hill, C.M. and Robinson, T. (1996), "Acquisition experience of UK firms in the former East Germany," *European Business Review*, Vol. 96, pp. 30-40.

Cote, K. (1990a), "Second-class citizens in their own country," *Advertising Age*, Vol. 61, p. 36.

Cote, K. (1990b), "West brands rain on East's parade: new Germany awash in new products," *Advertising Age*, Vol. 61, pp. 16, 51.

Coupey, E., Irwin, J.R. and Payne, J.W. (1998), "Product category familiarity and preference construction," *Journal of Consumer Research*, Vol. 24, pp. 459-68.

Creyer, E.H. and Ross Jr., W.T. (1997), "Tradeoffs between price and quality: how a value index affects preference formation," *Journal of Consumer Affairs*, Vol. 31, pp. 280-302.

Currim, I.S. and Schneider, L.G. (1991), "A taxonomy of consumer purchase strategies in a promotion intensive environment," *Marketing Science*, Vol. 10, pp. 91-110.

Dabholkar, P.A. (1994), "Incorporating choice into an attitudinal framework: analyzing models of mental comparison processes," *Journal of Consumer Research*, Vol. 21, pp. 100-18.

Dhar, R. (1997), "Consumer preference for a no-choice option," *Journal of Consumer Research*, Vol. 24, pp. 215-31.

Economist, The (2000), "Ten years of Germany," September 30.

Economist, The (2002), "A bubbly little tale: German wine," June 1.

Emcke, C. (1999), "Dolmetscher der Träume," *Der Spiegel*, Issue 39, http://www.spiegel.de

Ewing, J. (1999), "A nation still divided," *Business Week*, November 8, p. 70.

Feick, L. and Gierl, H. (1996), "Skepticism about advertising: a comparison of East and West German consumers," *International Journal of Research in Marketing*, Vol. 13, pp. 227-35.

GfK. (1997), *Der Verbraucher 1997*, Gesellschaft für Konsumentenforschung, http://www.gfk.cube.net

Granzin, K.L. and Olsen, J.E. (1998), "Americans' choice of domestic over foreign products: a matter of helping behavior?", *Journal of Business Research*, Vol. 43, pp. 39-54.

Gross, J.R., DeDee, J.K. and Swanson, S.R. (1993), "Customer attributes and their effect on service and product quality perceptions: an empirical study," *International Journal of Quality and Reliability Management*, Vol. 10, 14-24.

Grunert, K.G., Grunert, S.C., Glatzer, W. and Imkamp, H. (1995), "The changing consumer in Germany," *International Journal of Research in Marketing*, Vol. 12, 417-33.

Händel, W. (1991), "Switching systems in Eastern Germany," in Stern, S. (Ed.), *Meet United Germany*, FAZ Information Services, Frankfurt, pp. 100-9.

Han, C.M. (1988), "The role of consumer patriotism in the choice of domestic versus foreign products," *Journal of Advertising Research*, 28, pp. 25-32.

Hau, H. (1998), "Privatization under political influence: evidence from Eastern Germany," *European Economic Review*, Vol. 42, 1177-201.

Hinck, W. and Felix, R. (2000), "No quiero Taco Bell! An empirical investigation of Mexican consumer animosity toward U.S. products," paper presented at the Marketing in a Global Economy Conference, *American Marketing Association*, Buenos Aires, Argentina.

Holbrook, M.B. (1993), "Nostalgia and consumption preferences: some emerging patterns of consumer tastes," *Journal of Consumer Research*, Vol. 20, 245-56.

Howard, M. (1995), "An East German ethnicity? Understanding the new division of unified Germany," *German Politics and Society*, Vol. 13, pp. 49-70.

Huster, S. (2000), "Ost-Produkte im Westen chancenlos," *Rhein-Zeitung*, September 5, http://www.rhein-zeitung.de/archiv/

Januszewska, R. and Viane, J. (2001), "Acceptance of chocolate by preference cluster mapping across Belgium and Poland," *Journal of Euromarketing*, Vol. 11, pp. 61-86.

Kaynak, E. and Kara, A. (2001), "An examination of the relationship among consumer lifestyles, ethnocentrism, knowledge structures, attitudes and behavioural tendencies: a comparative study in two CIS states," *International Journal of Advertising*, Vol. 20, pp. 455-482.

Kaynak, E., Kucukemiroglu, O. and Hyder, A. (2000), "Consumers' country-of-origin (COO) perceptions of imported products in a homogenous less-developed country," *European Journal of Marketing*, Vol. 34, pp. 1221-41.

Kersting, S. (1997), "Neue Länder: Traditionsprodukte erobern ihren Platz in den Supermärkten zurück," *HB*, August 8, p. 7.

King, A.S., Samaras, S.A. and Ehrhard, B.J. (1996), Unification of Germany: doing business in the Eastern states," *International Journal of Management*, Vol. 13, pp. 33-42.

King, M.F. and Balasubramanian, S.K. (1994), "The effects of expertise, end goal, and product type on adoption of preference formation strategy," *Journal of the Academy of Marketing Science*, Vol. 22, pp. 146-59.

Kirkcaldy, B., Trimpop, R. and Furnham, A. (1999), "German unification: persistent differences between those from East and West," *Journal of Managerial Psychology*, Vol. 14, pp. 121-33.

Klein, J.B. (2002), "Us versus them, or us versus everyone? Delineating consumer aversion to foreign goods," *Journal of International Business Studies*, Vol. 33, pp. 345-363,

Klein, J.G. and Ettenson, R. (1999), "Consumer animosity and consumer ethnocentrism: an analysis of unique antecedents," *Journal of International Consumer Marketing*, Vol. 11, pp. 5-24.

Klein, J.G., Ettenson, R. and Morris, M.D. (1998), "The animosity model of foreign product purchase: an empirical test in the People's Republic of China," *Journal of Marketing*, Vol. 62, pp. 89-100.

La Roche, E. (1996), "Das Wiedererstehen der Grabower Küsse," *Tages-Anzeiger*, February 28: http://www.tages-anzeiger.ch

Lay, C. (1997), "Der Siegeszug der Ostprodukte," http://www.oeko-net.de/kommune/kommune1-97/tlay197.html

Lunze, U. (1996), "Es gibt ihn noch, den 'reinen' Ost-Rauch," *Frankenpost*, October 19, http://www.frankenpost.de

Lynch, D.J. (1999), "Glow is wearing off in the east," *USA Today*, October 11, pp. 1A-2A.

Macdonald, E.K. and Sharp, B.M. (2000), "Brand awareness effects on consumer decision making for a common, repeat purchase product: a replication," *Journal of Business Research*, Vol. 48, pp. 5-15.

Marcoux, J.-S., Filiatrault, P. and Cheron, E. (1997), "The attitudes underlying preferences of young urban educated Polish consumers towards products made in Western countries," *Journal of International Consumer Marketing*, Vol. 9, pp. 5-29.

Martell, M. (1996), "Geschmack erinnert an alte DDR-Zeiten," *Rhein-Zeitung*, August 13, http://www.rhein-zeitung.de/archiv/

Mazumdar, T. and Purushottam, P. (2000), "An investigation of reference price segments," *Journal of Marketing Research*, Vol. 37, pp. 246-58.

Mitchell, V.-W. (1999), "Consumer perceived risk: conceptualizations and models," *European Journal of Marketing*, Vol. 33, pp. 163-95.

Müller, B. (1996), "The Truth About Trabi," *Worldbusiness*, Vol. 2, p. 16.

Müller, U. (1997), "Der traumhafte Aufstieg der Rotkäppchen-Sektkellerei," *Die Welt*, February 6, http://www.welt.de

Nash, N.C. (1995), "A Wall in the Mind: rising Resentment in the East Divides Germany," *New York Times*, July 27, pp. D1-D2.

Nijssen, E.J., Douglas, S.P. and Bressers, P. (1999), "Attitudes towards foreign products: extending the animosity model," paper presented at the Second Biennial Joint Conference, *Academy of Marketing Science and American Marketing Association*, Stirling, Scotland.

Nill, A. (2001), "The policy of German (re)unification and implications for marketing and societal welfare," paper presented at the *American Marketing Association Winter Educators' Conference*, Scottsdale, Arizona.

Nowlis, S.M. and Simonson, I. (1997), "Attribute-task compatibility as a determinant of consumer preference reversals," *Journal of Marketing Research*, Vol. 34, 205-18.

Olsen, J.E., Granzin, K.L. and Biswas, A. (1993), "Influencing consumers' selection of domestic versus imported products: implications for marketing based on a model of helping behavior," *Journal of the Academy of Marketing Science*, Vol. 21, pp. 307-21.

Olshavsky, R.W., Aylesworth, A.B. and Kempf, D.S. (1995), "The price-choice relationship: a contingent processing approach," *Journal of Business Research*, Vol. 33, pp. 207-18.

Parnell, M.F. (1999), "Globalization, Eastern Germany and the 'Mittelstand,' " *European Business Review*, Vol. 99, pp. 32-41.

Posny, H. (1995), "Exoten-Produkt wahrt seine Chance," *Die Welt*, December 4, http://www.welt.de

Randlesome, C. (2000), "Changes in management culture and competencies: the German experience," *Journal of Management Development*, Vol. 19, pp. 629-642.

Rohnstock, K. (1996), Im Osten sieht man nichts Neues. *Die Welt*, August 16: http://www.welt.de

Scherhorn, G., Reisch, L.A. and Raab, G. (1990), "Addictive buying in West Germany: an empirical study," *Journal of Consumer Policy*, Vol. 13, pp. 355-87.

Schmoll, T. (1996), "Der Absatz im Westen hinkt," *Die Welt*, August 8, http://www.welt.de

Schopphoven, I. (1991), "Values and consumption patterns: a comparison between rural and urban consumers in Western Germany," *European Journal of Marketing*, Vol. 25, pp. 20-35.

Schröter, E. and Röber, M. (1997), "Regime change and administrative culture: role understandings and political attitudes of top bureaucrates from East and West Berlin," *American Review of Public Administration*, Vol. 27, pp. 107-32.

Sharma, S., Shimp, T.A. and Shin, J. (1995), "Consumer ethnocentrism: a test of antecedents and moderators," *Journal of the Academy of Marketing Science*, Vol. 23, pp. 26-37.

Siebert, H. (1991), "German unification: the economics of transition," *Economic Policy*, Vol. 13, pp. 287-340.

Stern, S. (1991), "Germanity-reflections on a people," in Stern, S. (Ed.), *Meet united Germany*, FAZ Information Services, Frankfurt, pp. 274-80.

Supphellen, M. and Rittenburg, T.L. (2001), "Consumer ethnocentrism when foreign products are better," *Psychology & Marketing*, Vol. 18, pp. 907-27.

Sweeney, E.P. and Hardaker, G. (1994), "The importance of organizational and national culture," *European Business Review*, Vol. 94, pp. 3-14.

Usunier, J.-C.G. (1991), "Business time perceptions and national cultures: a comparative survey," *Management International Review*, Vol. 31, 197-217.

Waldmann, M. (1990), "Wenn Filinchen, Esda und Komet Regale füllen, ist wieder Ostpro-Zeit," *Die Welt*, November 25, http://www.welt.de

Watson, J.J. and Wright, K. (2000), "Consumer ethnocentrism and attitudes toward domestic and foreign products," *European Journal of Marketing*, Vol. 34, pp. 1149-66.

Weber, S. (1991), "The cultural landscape," in Stern, S. (Ed.), *Meet United Germany*, FAZ Information Services, Frankfurt, pp. 262-73.

Willnecker, R. (1997), "Knödel, Cola, und geräucherte Eier," *Die Welt*, September 2, http://www.welt.de

Wittkowski, T.H. (2000), "Effects of animosity toward China on willingness to buy Chinese products," paper presented at the Ninth Annual World Business Congress, *International Management Development Association*, San Jose, Costa Rica.

Wydmusch, S. (2000), "The German churches after reunification," *Contemporary Review*, Vol. 277, pp. 321-28.

Ziamou, P., Zotos, Y., Lysonski, S., and Zafiropoulos, C. (1999), "Selling exports to consumers in Bulgaria: attitudes towards foreign products," *Journal of Euromarketing*, Vol. 7, pp. 59-77.

Zimmermann, E. (1998), "Ketten mit Boykott drohen," interview comments in *Rhein-Zeitung*, January 1, http://www.rhein-zeitung.de

Trade-Offs in Customer–Employee Focus: Implications on Boundary-Spanning Capabilities

Yelena Tsarenko
Felix T. Mavondo
Mark Gabbott
Graham Hooley
Gordon Greenly

SUMMARY. In pursuing their particular strategic goals, organisations place differential emphasis in their activities on employees and customers. Those who focus predominantly on employees see them as key re-

Yelena Tsarenko is Research Fellow, Department of Marketing, Monash University, P.O. Box 197, Caulfield East, VIC 3145, Australia (E-mail: Yelena.Tsarenko@ buseco.monash.edu.au). Felix T. Mavondo is Associate Professor, Department of Marketing, Monash University, Wellington Road, Clayton, VIC 3800, Australia (E-mail: Felix.Mavondo@buseco.monash.edu.au). Mark Gabbott is Professor, Head of Department, Department of Marketing, Monash University, P.O. Box 197, Caulfield East, VIC 3145, Australia (E-mail: Mark.Gabbott@buseco.monash.edu.au). Graham Hooley is Professor, Aston Business School, Aston University, United Kingdom (E-mail: g.j.hooley@aston.ac.uk). Gordon Greenly is Professor, Aston Business School, Aston University, United Kingdom (E-mail: g.e.greenley@aston.ac.uk).

Address correspondence to: Yelena Tsarenko, Research Fellow, Department of Marketing, Monash University, P.O. Box 197, Caulfield East, VIC 3145, Australia (E-mail: Yelena.Tsarenko@buseco.monash.edu.au).

[Haworth co-indexing entry note]: "Trade-Offs in Customer–Employee Focus: Implications on Boundary-Spanning Capabilities." Tsarenko, Yelena et al. Co-published simultaneously in *Journal of Euromarketing* (International Business Press, an imprint of The Haworth Press, Inc.) Vol. 14, No. 1/2, 2004, pp. 105-124; and: *Marketing Issues in Western Europe: Changes and Developments* (eds: Erdener Kaynak, and Frédéric Jallat) International Business Press, an imprint of The Haworth Press, Inc., 2004, pp. 105-124. Single or multiple copies of this article are available for a fee from The Haworth Document Delivery Service [1-800-HAWORTH, 9:00 a.m. - 5:00 p.m. (EST). E-mail address: docdelivery@haworthpress.com].

Digital Object Identifier: 10.1300/J037v14n01_06

sources contributing to successful achievement of goals, while those who focus on customers believe that customer commitment is the prime source of financial prosperity and competitive advantage. In all firms, there is potential for conflict and subsequent trade-offs in the emphasis placed on employee resources and customers. This paper investigates the implications of these potential trade-offs on firms' boundary-spanning capabilities (those capabilities that enable firms to interact effectively with their customers, their suppliers, their strategic allies and others in their business networks) in European and Australasian markets. The results suggest that those companies which achieve a strong but balanced focus on both employees and customers have heightened boundary-spanning capabilities. The comparison between UK and Australian businesses indicates that the balance is more highly developed in Australasian than European (UK) markets. *[Article copies available for a fee from The Haworth Document Delivery Service: 1-800-HAWORTH. E-mail address: <docdelivery@haworthpress.com> Website: <http://www.HaworthPress.com> © 2004 by The Haworth Press, Inc. All rights reserved.]*

KEYWORDS. Customer orientation, employee orientation, boundary-spanning capabilities

INTRODUCTION

Rapid and less predictable change in market environments, as exemplified by increased levels of competition, more rapid technological progress and globalization processes, has encouraged marketers to balance their traditional focus on long-term relationship with external customers, with an increased awareness of the importance of internal customers (employees) in achieving organizational goals (Berry, 1981). Internal marketing is gaining significant importance and is increasingly seen as a strategic route for organizations to build and sustain a competitive advantage over rivals. Based on the recognition that companies have two kinds of markets and customers (internal and external) (Piercy, 1995), we expanded previous research to investigate how organizations interact with their environment through their boundary spanning capabilities and activities. While many researchers have devoted attention to investigating the separate concepts of customer orientation and employee orientation, there is little examination of the dynamics associated with integrating the two concepts concurrently.

In highly uncertain, competitive and turbulent environments, this study explores the relationship between customer and employee orientation on a diverse set of boundary spanning capabilities in different cultural settings. Based on the notion that customer and employee orientated strategies lay the foundation for successful business operations (Brady & Jr Cronin, 2001; Deshpande, Farley, & Webster, 1993; Jaworski & Kohli, 1993), this study primarily focuses on the impact of these orientations on the development of particular capabilities and secondly aims to explore the similarities and differences that result from the configuration of customer and employee orientation across different regional markets–western Europe and Australasia.

The objective of the study is to understand the relationships between company focus (employee/customer trade-offs) and boundary spanning capabilities in these two different market regions. We compare the profiles of businesses in the UK and in Australia. The UK is an integral part of Western Europe, and a significant influence in the expanded Europe. As the Europe Union is expanded through the accession of ten additional states in April 2004 it becomes increasingly important to identify the sources of competitive advantage available to firms. The contrast with Australian firms is based on the recognition that Australia has close historical association with the UK in economic, political and social spheres and shares a common language. Hence differences between the UK and Australia are likely to be associated with differences in the market environment in which the firms operate (European and Australasian), rather than their cultural origins. We anticipate significant differences between the UK and Australian samples. If correct, these differences would suggest that the routes to competitive advantage and subsequent superior firm performance are different in European and Australasian markets.

ORGANISATIONAL FOCUS: CUSTOMERS AND EMPLOYEES

In recent years, the pivotal role of customers and employees has been acknowledged and empirically supported in the literature on organizational performance and corporate management (Fritz, 1996; Piercy, 1995; Varey & Lewis, 1999). Over the last decade the role of customers in all business processes has changed from relatively passive to active. Customers have become more demanding, sophisticated and knowledgeable. This has created new dynamics in supplier-customer interactions and presents new challenges to marketers. More and more organizations are focusing on issues of customer satisfaction and retention (Fornell, Johnson, Anderson, Cha, & Bryant, 1996) and this has significantly affected the behavior of members in many organizational networks.

There is marketing literature and significant evidence from business practice that supports the observation that customer-focused organizations achieve greater levels of business performance and success (Brady & Jr Cronin, 2001). However, there are a wide variety of views on the appropriate degree of customer orientation necessary to support business success. This can be viewed as lying on a continuum from loose to tight customer coupling and linkages (Danneels, 2003; Kellogg, 2000). These are two extremes that Danneels (2003) describes as the paradox for the organization in terms of keeping balance between understanding customer needs, establishing long-lasting relationships and flexibility and readiness to respond to emerging markets and breakthrough technologies. The question that inevitably arises is how to find and maintain the equilibrium that allows organizations to have distinctiveness, flexibility, adaptability and close interactions with customers? One of the solutions is the broadening of customer perspective by having greater awareness of other stakeholder interests that force organizations to more closely monitor the environmental changes (Meyer, 1982) and expand their range of market activities.

Focusing on customers, creating and delivering value for them is a prime goal of organization. However, the current business environment, characterized by technological and regulatory instability, ambiguous market signals, complicated structures and intense competition (Day, Schoemaker, & Gunther, 2000), places enormous pressure on employees who have to cope, deal and respond to all these challenges. Specifically, focusing on employees as internal customers expands the domain of business activity. The imperative is that employees should not only be informed about ". . . the organization's strategy, they must accurately understand the actions aligned with the strategy" (Boswell & Boudreau, 2001, p. 851). This is especially true for those employees performing interactive roles between the organization and the business environment. They are often referred to as boundary spanners (Bowen & Schneider, 1985; Stamper & Johlke, 2003), since they operate at the interface between organizations and environment. Their work includes interaction with customers through addressing their often highly variable, complex, and distinctive needs. On the other hand, they represent the interests of their organization. This dual role leads to the creation uncertainty, role ambiguity, role stress and conflict in their daily activities (Stamper & Johlke, 2003).

The degree to which organizations consider and focus on employee needs, the attraction, retention and motivation of skilled people, clear communication and organizational responsiveness constitutes what we term employee orientation (Varey & Lewis, 1999). This is viewed as an organization's concentration of efforts on value creation for internal customers. Providing superior value to the external customer is associated with successful management of employees in terms of paying close attention to their needs and requirements (Conduit & Mavondo, 2001). Employee orientation denotes the firm's willingness to invest time and resources in staff development potentially leading to superior skills and knowledge in support of customer service. These skills could lead to the "ability to perform individual functions more effectively" or high adaptability to "changes in market environment" (Day & Wensley, 1988). Employee orientation involves a range of activities such as training and education, providing opportunities for greater income and paying attention to professional growth (Papasolomou-Doukakis, 2002). Thus, fundamental to employee orientation is the compatibility of organizational and individual goals (Jauch, Osborn, & Terpening, 1980).

Despite the fact that the literature widely supports a focus on employees as one of the most valuable assets in achieving and maintaining overall satisfactory organizational performance and as an important complement to external marketing programs (Piercy & Morgan, 1991), in reality, organizations differ in the form of relationship they develop with employees. It is acknowledged that organizations which pay close attention to the wants and needs of their employees are "more likely to explicate work norms and expectations, thus directly reducing the amount of conflict and ambiguity associated with various employee roles" (Stamper & Johlke, 2003, p. 581).

The underlying consideration in focusing on the two major assets of organizations as customers and employees was determined by so called "cycle of capability." This viewpoint states that there is a reinforcing effect between satisfied customers and satisfied employees (Heskett, Sasser Jr, & Schlesinger, 1997). Piercy (1995) integrated internal and external customer satisfaction for developing successful marketing strategies, relationship marketing and sustainable business performance. Using the typology of customer-employee orientation analogous to the one developed by Piercy (1995) we employ the framework which enables insights into how organizational configuration on employee and customer orientation might have implications for the development of boundary spanning capabilities. The quadrants in the conceptual framework imply that organizations can be highly committed simultaneously to both customer and employee orientation (HH), or be poor at both (LL), or to place more emphasis on customers (HcLe) or employee orientation (LcHe). The horizontal axis represents the degree of customer orientation and the vertical one is the degree to which the company is employee oriented. (See Figure 1.)

> *Proposition 1: Organisations with different degrees of focus on customers and employees will have differences in their boundary spanning capabilities.*

BOUNDARY-SPANNING CAPABILITIES

The resource-based view of the firm considers organizations as bundles of assets and capabilities (Hooley et al., 1999). Using a resource-based view we investigate the implications of customer orientation-employee orientation profiles on a business's portfolio of capabilities. Building on research on boundary spanning capabilities in general we identify the set of specific capabilities as a bundle of strategic activities which reflect the distinctive deployment of resources and require high customer and employee asset involvement.

Strategic Alliances Capabilities

The role of strategic alliances has been significantly increased with growth in competition in business markets. The explosion in the number of alliances is associated with gaining access to new markets, products, partners' resources and expertise more quickly and at lower costs to achieve mutual benefits and to improve the competitive advantage of all involved parties (Drago, 1997; Lambe, Spekman, & Hunt, 2002).

FIGURE 1. Conceptual Representation of the Matrix of Customer Orientation and Employee Orientation

	Customer Focus	
Employee Focus	Low	High
High	HeLc	HH
Low	LL	LeHc

Forming strategic alliances organizations aim to reduce the duplication of resources and efforts and eliminate environmental contingency namely external and internal uncertainty (Burgers, Hill, & Kim, 1993; Drago, 1997). The environmental uncertainty extends from gaining access to new markets, suppliers and customers to sharing tangible and intangible resources such as information and knowledge. Organizational uncertainty is related to scarcity of resources and lack of information and knowledge required for successful operation (Drago, 1997). It was noted that when uncertainty is high, organizations interact more, not less, with external parties in order to access both knowledge and resources (Powell, 1998).

Integration through strategic alliances represents the strategic orientation in the firm's thinking and approach rather than combined resource, shared stakes and expanded joint capabilities (Johnson, 1999). Alliances represent the partnership between people, "who together form a new informal or formal organization" (Leisen, Lilly, & Winsor, 2002, p. 202) and these relationships represent ties which go beyond formal contractual agreement. As Powell (1998) stated, the interaction between employees is replaced by higher form such as collaboration which brings all members together to work on the cutting edge of creating a new service or developing a new product or process (Hefner, 1994). Very often such tasks are performed through collaborations with people from other organizations (Daboub & Calton, 2002). Employees are one of the key aspects required for the strategic alliances to be successful. Apart from being flexible and able to deal efficiently with ambiguity they "should be recognized for the risks they assume in participating and developing strategic alliances" (Hefner, 1994).

> *H1: Strategic alliance capability is expected to vary HH > HeLc > LeHc > LL*

Networking Capabilities

Networking capabilities represent the ability to create trust and commitment between partners, as well as sharing expertise and more tangible assets (Hooley, Greenly, Fahy, & Cadogan, 2001). These capabilities rest on commitment-trust theory (Morgan & Hunt, 1994).

Success in networking capabilities stems from the ability to establish relationships, get access to information and decision support systems, and maintain these relationships. "A key network characteristic is being flexible and adaptable to change" (Piercy & Cravens, 1995, p. 18) and expand team building skills. One of the claimed advantages of networks is the access by all members to informational and other resources that allows them to "improve abilities to deliver quality and services to the customers" (Piercy & Cravens, 1995, p. 27).

However, at the same time multiple partnerships and expansion network in membership may result in not all members sharing and valuing external customer needs and being more focused on creating value for internal customers. Since all departments in organizations have their own internal and external customers, development of networking capabilities is served as a means to coordinate interdepartmental transactions and relationships. The organization becomes responsible for all individuals in different departments and their relationship with customers when providing them with quality services (Lings, 2000). The networking capabilities drive generation, synthesis, and distribution of ideas (Powell, 1998), therefore, the success of the organization depends on its interaction and cooperation with partners.

Because the success of networking capabilities depends on people's willingness to work across functions and organizations, we hypothesize that employee orientation will have a greater impact on networking capabilities.

H2: Networking capabilities are expected to vary: HH > HeLc > LeHc > LL

Relationship Management Capabilities

Considering relationship management as a separate aspect of network models is substantiated by the fact that "network organization is about not only structural upheaval, but also a new managerial ethos" (Achrol & Kotler, 1999). It is the ability to manage relationships with all stakeholders, i.e., people "who are or may become material in assisting the [entrepreneur] to progress the growth ambitions of the enterprise" (Hill, McGowan, & Drummond, 1999). While some organizations might be skilled and effective in initiating alliances and linkages in the supply chain, some will have greater capabilities in managing relationships leading to superior rewards. The different groups of stakeholders forming the networks are not self-sustaining, they require considerable investment, thus the focus of relationship management is on developing mutuality, commitment, trust and effective communication with all parties involved. A relationship management strategy can be a source of competitiveness when organizations create special atmosphere and internal culture in which all employees deal with different actors in the network based on integrative strategy, presenting the organization's value, credibility and commitments in the different settings. Currently the dominant theme in the literature on relationship management is finding such factors which can move the relationship from transactional interactions to long-term relationships (Hewett, Money, & Sharma, 2002).

The management approach aimed at building and maintaining long-term beneficial relationships with customers has gained significant priority and acceptance in business practice (Gruen, Summers, & Acito, 2000). Relationship management perspective implies that the emphasis on the process of interaction between organization and customers moves from responsiveness to dialogue mode where customers are actively involved in shaping business processes on different levels (product design, methods of payment, ordering and delivery mode) (Berthon, Hulbert, & Pitt, 1999). Consequently we hypothesize that customer orientation will be dominant in developing these capabilities.

> *H3: Relationship management capability is expected to vary: HH >*
> *LeHc > HeLc > LL*

Inside-Out Capabilities

While often not explicitly considered as marketing capabilities, strong financial management, effective human resource management, and operations management skills can be a critical base for delivering customer value and hence achieving market and financial objectives of the firm. Inside-out capabilities characterize the relationship of many organizations to the outside world (Day, 1994). Organizations solve the internal contradictions internally and then, from this experience, begin to focus on the outside world (Hooley et al., 1999). This perspective is consistent with a strong focus on internal processes with occasional interest in the external environment. Such capabilities are especially effective in improving operating systems. Because of the internal focus we expect inside-out capabilities to be highly employee dependent, therefore:

> *H4: Inside-out capability is expected to vary: HH > HeLc > LeHc > LL*

Outside-In Capabilities

These are often considered the most critical marketing capabilities. They include the ability, developed through both formal and informal market research, to understand customer wants and needs and hence align the organization's offerings to meet customer needs (Day, 1994; Hooley et al., 1999). While there is some indication that paying special attention to customers may be disadvantageous (Danneels, 2003), received theory and conventional wisdom suggests otherwise (Kohli & Jaworski, 1990; Narver & Slater, 1990). Customers and other stakeholders are critical as potential sources of information, innovation, word-of-mouth communication and sources of referrals. An organization with outside-in capabilities is able to bring in and harness external information important for organizational success. The issue is that some companies are very effective at using external information such as market research findings, customer and other stakeholder information. This results in significant improvement of both internal and external relationships. We posit these capabilities as the alternative to inside-out (Day, 1994; Hooley et al., 2001; Kay, 1993). This leads us to the hypothesis:

H5: Outside-in capability will vary: HH > LeHc > HeLc > LL

Supply Chain Management Capabilities

Supply chain management is one of the most popular concepts in management (Svendsen, 1998) and is based on channel integration and cooperation to minimize costs while delivering greatest net value to the ultimate customers (Langley & Holcomb, 1992; Pelton, Strutton, & Lumpkin, 2002). The ability to develop and support an economically efficient channel operation can be enhanced by establishing trusting and ethically oriented forms of partnership between members, thereby bolstering the collective market strength and producing a significant competitive advantage.

Supply chain capabilities are complex and diverse. They include capabilities in identifying and selecting appropriate partners, negotiating win-win situations, maintaining and sustaining the relationship over time. These capabilities are based on a buyer-supplier framework or trading relationships. Effective working with partners and managing the channel relationships may be part of corporate culture and its role may facilitate or hinder these relationships (McAfee, Glassman, & Honeycutt Jr, 2002). Close working with channel members brings benefits, but at a cost. Relationships have the potential to bring tensions such as "excessive demands being made by the buyer, which are passed down to employees who, among other things, are in turn under severe pressure to deliver enhanced quality in a shorter time" (McHugh, Humphreys, & McIvor, 2003, p. 17). McAfee, Glassman and Honeycutt (2002) note there are two aspects in channel relationships that should be considered: (1) the internal culture that characterizes employee expectations and behavior; (2) the external culture that characterizes channel members' expectations and behavior. This suggests that employees are a crucial investment of the organization in terms of their selecting, training and educating in pursuing "win-win" strategies with partners in the channel. We postulate that employee orientation will have stronger implications for supply chain management capabilities. Hence:

H6: Supply chain capability is expected to vary: HH > HeLc > LeHc > LL

METHODOLOGY

This paper reports results from studies conducted concurrently in the UK and Australia. Following in-depth interviews with 20 senior marketing executives in the UK to develop scales to measure employee orientation, customer orientation and boundary spanning capabilities, a questionnaire was developed and pilot tested. After minor modification, this was then adopted as a core questionnaire in both countries for administration by mail. In both countries, sampling frames were provided through Dunn and Bradstreet using similar industrial classifications. The eight page questionnaires were mailed to businesses in Australia and the UK, addressed to the Chief Marketing Executive in each. In Australia, a total sample of 251 usable responses (response rate 12%) consisting of mostly Business Services (22%) and Manufacturing sub-sectors (41%) was obtained. Small to medium sized companies with fewer than 200 employees dominate respondent firms (66%). In the UK 485 usable responses (a 10% response rate) were received. Of these, Business Services accounted for 25% of responses and manufacturing firms 41%, similar to the Australian sample. Size breaks were assessed differently in the UK, with 70% of firms falling in the under 300 employee category.

Non-response bias was tested through comparing means on the different constructs between early and late respondents (Armstrong & Overton, 1977). In Australia first half respondents were compared with second half respondents. In the UK first third respondents were compared with last third. No significant differences were found using t-tests at the .05 level, providing some confidence that non-response bias was not a problem in this study. Obtained data represents the wide variety in terms of industry sectors and size of the organizations.

Measurements

Customer focus. We utilized the six item, seven-point scale developed by Narver and Slater (1990) as one of three components of market orientation to measure customer orientation. Overall customer orientation was calculated as the mean value across the six items. Businesses were allocated to either low or high depending on whether the score of customer orientation was below or above 2.5. The reliability of customer orientation was Cronbach $\alpha = 0.79$.

Employee focus was measured using four indicators developed from the literature and in-depth interviews. The procedure employed to identify low and high degree of employee orientation was similar to that for customer orientation. The reliability of employee orientation was Cronbach $\alpha = 0.78$.

The boundary-spanning capabilities were also developed from the literature (most notably the work of Day, 1994 and Piercy and Cravens, 1995). Separate scales were developed for each type of capability. These were assessed for their psychometric properties and found all to have Chronbach's α exceeding 0.70 recommended by Nunnally (1978) indicating high levels of internal reliability.

Four classifications of firms, following Figure 1, were used to evaluate the implications of each combined focus on boundary spanning capabilities in Australia and in the UK. The findings were then compared across the two countries to see if there were significant differences.

RESULTS AND DISCUSSION

The results for the UK and Australian samples showed few differences, hence, they will be discussed together but where differences do emerge they will be highlighted. However, it should be noted that the level of the scores are much higher for the Australian sample than for the UK sample.

Differences Across Configurations

Strategic alliance capabilities. This hypothesis (H1) is partially supported, however the only significant difference is between HH and LL in the Australian and UK samples. Organizations with a HH configuration had stronger strategic alliance capabilities than those with LL configuration. There are no differences between the two non-symmetrical groups (HeLc and HcLe) suggesting that either orientation is a substitute for the other. This is surprising since one would have anticipated a stronger association between strategic alliance capabilities and employee orientation.

Networking capabilities. This hypothesis (H2) is also partly supported, however the HeLc has a lower score than LeHc contrary to expectation, although the differences are not statistically significant. Networking capabilities refer to a bundle of capabilities that organizations require for effective operation. Networking capabilities can be built by employees in their interactions with customers, competitors, suppliers, etc. A strong customer orientation can lead to transforming the relationship with customers beyond transactions. Customers can become important sources of new product ideas, competitor information, word of mouth recommendation, etc. This implies that networking capabilities are more strongly associated with customer orientation than with employee orientation. These results suggest emphasis on customers leads to better networking capabilities. The pattern of the scores is the same across the two countries.

Relationship management capabilities. This hypothesis (H3) is largely supported. HH is significantly different and superior to the other configurations and LeHc is significantly greater than LL. The HeLc has a lower score than LeHc according to expectations but the differences are not statistically significant. This implies that relationship management capabilities are more strongly related to customer orientation than to employee orientation. The pattern of the scores is similar across the two countries.

Inside-out capabilities. Hypothesis (H4) is not supported in both the UK and Australian samples. The implication is that internally generated capabilities require an external relevance and customer input to be effective.

Outside-in capabilities. Hypothesis (H5) is supported and there are significant differences indicating that HH and LeHc configurations have higher scores than LL. These results seem to suggest that if the trade-off between customer orientation and employee orientation was necessary (rather than achieving balance), priority should be given to customer orientation. If both can be achieved at a reasonable cost, the HH configuration would be the most effective.

Supply chain capabilities. Hypothesis (H6) is not supported, indicating that the differences across the configurations are not significant. Probably this suggests that respondents felt that there was mutual need and no asymmetric investment was required to build or sustain supply chain capabilities. It suggests these capabilities are considered important, irrespective of the configuration of the business.

Regression Analysis and Identification of Model Type

Results in the last two columns in Tables 1 and 2 were testing the regressions of employee focus, customer orientation and their interaction as determinants of boundary spanning capabilities. The intent was to establish if there were significant interaction effects. The model tested was of the form:

TABLE 1. Differences in Boundary Spanning Capabilities and Variance Explained by the Model (Australia)

Variable	Means Australia						R^2	Adjusted R^2
	LL N = 51	HeLc N = 33	LeHc N = 51	HH N = 115	F-ratio	Difference		
Strategic alliances capabilities	2.98	3.17	3.12	3.34	4.48*	HH > LL	.052	.040
Networking capabilities	2.93	3.22	3.34	3.52	9.88***	HH > HeLc & LL LeHc > LL	.108	.097
Relationship management capabilities	3.50	3.76	3.95	4.25	17.69***	HH > LeHc & HeLc & LL LeHc > LL	.177	.167
Inside-out capabilities	3.29	3.55	3.72	3.76	7.72***	HH & LeHc > LL	.086	.075
Outside-in capabilities	3.49	3.71	3.97	3.89	7.44***	HH & LeHc > LL	.083	.072
Supply chain capabilities	3.25	3.34	3.34	3.44	1.49		.018	.006

TABLE 2. Differences in Boundary Spanning Capabilities and Variance Explained by the Model (UK)

Variables	Means UK						R^2	Adjusted R^2
	LL N = 84	HeLc N = 95	LeHc N = 73	HH N = 195	F-ratio	Difference		
Strategic alliances capabilities	2.93	3.07	3.12	3.15	3.18**	HH > LL	.021	.014
Networking capabilities	3.04	3.22	3.32	3.30	6.26***	HH & LeHc & HeLc > LL	.041	.034
Relationship management capabilities	3.31	3.83	4.05	4.36	63.76***	HH > LeHc & HeLc & LL	.302	.297
Inside-out capabilities	3.24	3.42	3.56	3.68	13.02***	HH & LeHc > LL & HeLc	.081	.075
Outside-in capabilities	3.46	3.66	3.91	3.96	16.42***	HH & LeHc > LL	1.00	.094
Supply chain capabilities	3.14	3.17	3.26	3.28	2.53		.017	.010

$$Y = \alpha + \beta_1 \text{Customer Orientation} + \beta_2 \text{Employees Orientation} + \beta_3 \text{Customer*Employee}$$

Where: Y = the boundary spanning capabilities.

In all the models the coefficients for customer orientation and employee orientation were significant at least at $p < .001$ and for all the boundary spanning activities the coefficient of the interaction term (β_3) were $p > .10$. These results confirm that the effect model (Joyce, Slocum, & Ginlow, 1982) was the most appropriate. This supports the notion that "more is better," i.e., organizations should seek to develop more of both employee and customer orientation since there are no significant interaction effects. The R^2 value (proportion of the variance in the boundary spanning capabilities explained by the model) were generally low suggesting that customer orientation and employee orientation do not account for significant levels of the variance of the boundary spanning capabilities.

Comparison of Differences Between Configurations in UK and Australia

We attempted to compare similar configurations across the two countries, i.e., LL in Australia against LL in the UK, etc. To our surprise the LL, HeLc and LeHc configurations did not show any statistical differences. Differences were observed for the HH configuration and the results are in Table 3. These results indicate that Australian respondents have significantly higher scores for supply chain capabilities (p < .01), for strategic alliance (p < .01) and networking capabilities (p < .001). In other words Australian businesses oriented towards establishing and maintaining these boundary spanning capabilities consider both high customer and employee orientation as integral to their high achievements and satisfactory business performance. This is due to the existence of a few developed countries and many developing. This creates certain market instability and places more demands for achieving sustainability through all forms of relationships (network, supply chain and strategic alliance). In comparison, Western European has its own peculiarities but at least most of the economies are comparable in their stage of development.

There were no significant differences for inside-out or outside-in capabilities and relationship management capabilities. Assuming scale equivalence, the implications are that boundary spanning capabilities may be more important in Australia than in the UK. This could be accounted for by the geographic factors such as low density and huge distances that separate Australian businesses as compared to the UK.

CONCLUSIONS

From these results two main conclusions can be drawn. First, in order to build strong and effective boundary-spanning capabilities, businesses

TABLE 3. Differences Between UK and Australian Businesses with Similar HH Configuration

Variable	Australia	UK	Difference
Strategic alliances capabilities	3.34	3.15	−2.88***
Networking capabilities	3.52	3.30	−3.21***
Relationship management capabilities	4.25	4.35	1.64 (ns)
Inside-out capabilities	3.76	3.68	−1.18 (ns)
Outside-in capabilities	3.89	3.96	1.06 (ns)
Supply chain capabilities	3.44	3.28	−2.60**

need to pursue a balanced but intense focus both on their customers and their employees. The development and maintenance of effective boundary spanning capabilities requires both a commitment to employees and a customer orientation, and these attributes are not even partial substitutes of each other. The most effective configuration in both the Australian and UK samples is the HH. The LL configuration is, predictably, the least effective. Given the potential trade-offs that exist in many firms; the next most effective configuration to the HH is the LeHc configuration. This suggests customer orientation is to be pursued more vigorously than employee orientation. This conclusion is counter-intuitive in that the theory and conceptualization of capabilities suggest that the internal dynamics of any business are the true sources of competitive advantage.

This study indicates that employee orientation and customer orientation are important organizational approaches in both the UK and Australia. The results further indicate there are no differences in the boundary spanning capabilities of businesses other than at the HH configuration. This shows a consistency of results across countries. At the HH configuration, Australian companies have significantly higher boundary spanning capabilities and this can be accounted for by wide dispersion of businesses in Australia. As Europe expands eastwards to take in former planned economies, a greater focus on boundary spanning activities may be required of UK companies.

These results may be confounded in suggesting that customer orientation is more important than employee orientation. This is because of the intense and continuous interaction between employees and customers. This may result in formal and informal information being captured by employees, and employee orientation may be a mediating factor in transmitting the effects of customer orientation. This cautions us to consider employees as perhaps the most important internal asset of any business.

Finally, both customer orientation and employee orientation are important and deserve investment to cope with environmental dynamics and manage organisation-environment interface. The implication for managers is that where they are faced with a trade-off between customer orientation and employee orientation, it would be better to give greater weight to customer orientation as this appears to be more effective across all boundary spanning activities.

REFERENCES

Achrol, R. S., & Kotler, P. (1999). Marketing in the Network Economy. *Journal of Marketing*, *63*(Special issue 1999), 146-163.

Armstrong, S. J., & Overton, T. S. (1977). Estimating Nonresponse Bias in Mail Surveys. *Journal of Marketing Research*, *14*(3), 396-402.

Berry, L. L. (1981). The Employee as Customer. *Journal of Retail Banking*, *3*(1), 33-40.

Berthon, P., Hulbert, J. M., & Pitt, L. F. (1999). To Serve or Create? Strategic Orientations Toward Customers and Innovation. *California Management Review*, *42*(1), 37-58.

Boswell, W. R., & Boudreau, J. W. (2001). How leading companies create, measure and achieve strategic results through "line of sight." *Management Decision*, *39*(10), 851-859.

Bowen, D. E., & Schneider, B. (1985). Boundary-Spanning Role Employees and the Service Encounter: Some Guidelines for Management and Research. In J. A. Czepiel & M. R. Solomon & C. F. Surprenant (Eds.), *The Service Encounter: Managing employee/customer interaction in service businesses* (pp. 127-147). Lexington, MA: D.C. Heath.

Brady, M. K., & Jr Cronin, J. J. (2001). Customer Orientation Effects on Customer Service Perceptions and Outcome Behaviors. *Journal of Service Research*, *3*(3), 241-251.

Burgers, W. P., Hill, C. W., & Kim, W. C. (1993). A theory of global strategic alliances: the case of the global auto industry. *Strategic Management Journal*, *14*(6), 419-432.

Conduit, J., & Mavondo, F. T. (2001). How critical is internal customer orientation to market orientation? *Journal of Business Research*, *51*(1), 11-24.

Daboub, A. J., & Calton, J. M. (2002). Stakeholder learning dialogues: How to preserve ethical responsibility in Networks. *Journal of Business Ethics; JBE*, *41*(Nov/Dec), 85-98.

Danneels, E. (2003). Tight-loose coupling with customers: the enactment of customer orientation. *Strategic Management Journal*, *24*(6), 559-576.

Day, G. S. (1994). The Capabilities of Market-Driven Organizations. *Journal of Marketing*, *58*(4), 37-52.

Day, G. S., Schoemaker, P. J. H., & Gunther, R. E. (Eds.). (2000). *Wharton on managing emerging technologies*. New York: Chichester: Wiley.

Day, G. S., & Wensley, R. (1988). Assessing advantage: A framework for diagnosing competitive superiority. *Journal of Marketing*, *52*(April), 1-20.

Deshpande, R., Farley, J. W., & Webster, F. E., Jr. (1993). Corporate Culture, Customer Orientation, and Innovativeness in Japanese Firms: A Quadrad Analysis. *Journal of Marketing*, *57*(1), 23-37.

Drago, W. A. (1997). When strategic alliances make sense. *Industrial Management & Data Systems* (2), 53-57.

Fornell, C., Johnson, M. D., Anderson, E. W., Cha, J., & Bryant, B. E. (1996). The American Customer Satisfaction Index: Nature, purpose, and findings. *Journal of Marketing*, *60*(Oct), 7-18.

Fritz, W. (1996). Market Orientation and Corporate Success: Findings from Germany. *European Journal of Marketing, 30*(8), 59-74.

Gruen, T. W., Summers, J. O., & Acito, F. (2000). Relationship marketing activities, commitment, and membership behaviors in professional associations. *Journal of Marketing, 64*(Jul), 34-49.

Hefner, L. L. (1994). Strategic alliances and the human resource implications for records managers. *ARMA Records Management Quarterly, 28*(Jul), 13.

Heskett, J. L., Sasser Jr, W. E., & Schlesinger, L. A. (1997). *The service profit chain: How leading companies link profit and growth to loyalty, satisfaction, and value.* New York: Free Press.

Hewett, K., Money, R. B., & Sharma, S. (2002). An exploration of the moderating role of buyer corporate culture in industrial buyer-seller relationships. *Journal of the Academy of Marketing Science, 30*(3), 229-239.

Hill, J., McGowan, P., & Drummond, P. (1999). The development and application of a qualitative approach to researching the marketing networks of small firm entrepreneurs. *Qualitative Market Research, 2*(2), 71-81.

Hooley, G., Fahy, J., Cox, T., Beracs, J., Fonfara, K., & Snoj, B. (1999). Marketing capabilities and firm performance: A hierarchical model. *Journal of Market Focused Management, 4*(3), 259-278.

Hooley, G., Greenly, G., Fahy, J., & Cadogan, J. (2001). Market-focused resources, competitive positioning and firm performance. *Journal of Marketing Management, 17*(2-6), 503-520.

Jauch, L., Osborn, R. N., & Terpening, W. D. (1980). Goal congruence and employee orientations: The substitution effect. *Academy of Management Journal, 23*(3), 544-550.

Jaworski, B. J., & Kohli, A. K. (1993). Market Orientation: Antecedents and Consequences. *Journal of Marketing, 57*(3), 53-70.

Johnson, J. L. (1999). Strategic integration in industrial distribution channels: Managing the interfirm relationship as a strategic asset. *Journal of the Academy of Marketing Science, 27*(1), 4-18.

Joyce, W., Slocum, J., & Ginlow, M. (1982). Person situation and interaction: Competing models of fit. *Journal of Occupational Behavior, 3*(4), 256-280.

Kay, J. (1993). The structure of strategy. *Business Strategy Review, 4*(2), 17-37.

Kellogg, D. L. (2000). A customer contact measurement model: An extension. *International Journal of Service Industry Management, 11*(1), 26-45.

Kohli, A. K., & Jaworski, B. J. (1990). Market Orientation: The Construct, Research Propositions, and Managerial Implications. *Journal of Marketing, 54*(2), 1-18.

Lambe, C. J., Spekman, R. E., & Hunt, S. D. (2002). Alliance Competence, Resources and Alliance Success: Conceptualisation, Measurement, and Initial Test. *Journal of the Academy of Marketing Science, 30*(2), 141-158.

Langley, C. J. J., & Holcomb, M. C. (1992). Creating logistics customer value. *Journal of Business Logistics, 13*(2), 1-28.

Leisen, B., Lilly, B., & Winsor, R. D. (2002). The effects of organisational culture and market orientation on the effectiveness of strategic marketing alliances. *Journal of Services Marketing, 16*(3), 201-222.

Lings, I. N. (2000). Internal marketing and supply chain management. *Journal of Services Marketing, 14*(1), 27-43.

McAfee, R. B., Glassman, M., & Honeycutt Jr, E. D. (2002). The effects of culture and human resource management policies on supply chain management strategy. *Journal of Business Logistics, 23*(1), 1-18.

McHugh, M., Humphreys, P., & McIvor, R. (2003). Buyer-supplier relationships and organizational health. *Journal of Supply Chain Management, 39*(Spring), 15-25.

Meyer, A. D. (1982). Adapting to environmental jolts. *Administrative Science Quarterly, 24*(7), 515-537.

Morgan, R., & Hunt, S. (1994). The Commitment-Trust Theory of Relationship Marketing. *Journal of Marketing, 58*(July), 20-38.

Narver, J. C., & Slater, S. F. (1990). The effect of a market orientation on business profitability. *Journal of Marketing, 54*(4), 20-36.

Papasolomou-Doukakis, I. (2002). The role of employee development in customer relations: The case of UK retail banks. *Corporate Communications: An international journal, 7*(1), 62-76.

Pelton, L. E., Strutton, D., & Lumpkin, J. R. (2002). *Marketing Channels: A relationship management approach.* McGraw-Hill.

Piercy, N. F. (1995). Customer Satisfaction and the Internal Market: Marketing our Customers to our Employees. *Journal of Marketing Practice: Applied Marketing Science, 1*(1), 22-44.

Piercy, N. F., & Cravens, D. W. (1995). The network paradigm and marketing organisation. *European Journal of Marketing, 29*(3), 7-34.

Piercy, N. F., & Morgan, N. A. (1991). Internal Marketing–The Missing Half of the Marketing Programme. *Long Range Planning, 24*(2), 82-93.

Powell, W. W. (1998). Learning from collaboration: Knowledge and networks in the biotechnology and pharmaceutical industries. *California Management Review, 40*(Spring), 228-240.

Stamper, C. L., & Johlke, M. C. (2003). The Impact of Perceived Organizational Support on the Relationship Between Boundary Spanner Role Stress and Work Outcomes. *Journal of Management, 29*(4), 569-588.

Svendsen, A. (1998). *The stakeholder strategy.* San Francisco: Berrett-Koehler Publishers, Inc.

Varey, R. J., & Lewis, B. R. (1999). A broadened conception of internal marketing. *European Journal of Marketing, 33*(9/10), 926-944.

Price Strategy in the EU: Suggestions to Chinese Exporters in the Light of Anti-Dumping

Jørgen Ulff-Møller Nielsen

SUMMARY. This paper investigates the EU anti-dumping policy towards Chinese companies. Based on this analysis, the paper presents practical advice to Chinese or foreign managers in companies in China with export to the EU. Firstly, the CELEX database may give some important information on how to formulate a price policy for exports to the EU in order to avoid anti-dumping measures. Secondly, the owner structure of the company is important, if market economy status with its lower duties, is wanted. Wholly owned foreign companies or joint ventures with a majority of foreign capital seem to have the biggest probability of achieving market economy status. Generally, evidence of independence of the Chinese public authorities is important. Thirdly, owner structure also counts in relation to getting individual treatment; here especially, freedom in exporting is decisive. Fourthly, if an anti-dumping investigation seems to be against the interests of the com-

Jørgen Ulff-Møller Nielsen is Associate Professor, Department of International Business, Aarhus School of Business, Fuglesangs Allé 4, 8210 Aarhus V, Denmark (E-mail: JUM@asb.dk).

[Haworth co-indexing entry note]: "Price Strategy in the EU: Suggestions to Chinese Exporters in the Light of Anti-Dumping." Nielsen, Jørgen Ulff-Møller. Co-published simultaneously in *Journal of Euromarketing* (International Business Press, an imprint of The Haworth Press, Inc.) Vol. 14, No. 1/2, 2004, pp. 125-143; and: *Marketing Issues in Western Europe: Changes and Developments* (eds: Erdener Kaynak, and Frédéric Jallat) International Business Press, an imprint of The Haworth Press, Inc., 2004, pp. 125-143. Single or multiple copies of this article are available for a fee from The Haworth Document Delivery Service [1-800-HAWORTH, 9:00 a.m. - 5:00 p.m. (EST). E-mail address: docdelivery@haworthpress.com].

pany, it should make an offer to the EU Commission to raise its export prices instead of paying duty. *[Article copies available for a fee from The Haworth Document Delivery Service: 1-800-HAWORTH. E-mail address: <docdelivery@haworthpress.com> Website: <http://www.HaworthPress.com> © 2004 by The Haworth Press, Inc. All rights reserved.]*

KEYWORDS. EU anti-dumping policy, owner structure, market economy status, individual treatment, price strategies, circumvention of duties

INTRODUCTION

In the beginning of 21st century we can look back at the last 10 to 15 years as a period with very radical changes in the world economy. Not only the transition of the former communist countries in Europe from planned to market economies, but also the beginning of a transition process in the most populous economy of the world, China, have been significantly changed. Even though the political system as such has not changed much in China, its economic structures are changing at a rapid pace. Parallel to these transitional processes, globalisation is certainly increasingly on the agenda–partly as a result of technological changes (the cost of spreading knowledge has fallen drastically) and partly as a result of a consciously multilateral trade and investment liberalisation process (leading to the creation of the WTO in 1995).

Along these trends we have experienced an extensive increase in regional economic integration (free trade areas, customs unions, etc.) all over the world, with the deepest integration taking place in the EU, through the creation of the Single Market (1994) and the Euro (1999).

But there is no rose without a thorn. Whatever trade and investment liberalisation strategy a country decides to follow, it always wants to guard itself against unforeseeable circumstances by building a trade policy readiness. Therefore, the overall liberalisation trend does not necessarily provide an accurate picture of the degree of protectionism in the world–especially not for a country like China, that until the end of 2001, was neither a member of WTO nor participating in a regional club.

The overall objective of this paper is to give advice to Chinese companies in formulating export price strategies when they are exposed to the risks of contingent protection in foreign markets. A "Chinese" company (in relation to anti-dumping legislation) is defined as a company with production facilities in China–whether it is a state- or privately-owned domestic Chinese company, a joint venture between a domestic Chinese and a foreign company or a wholly foreign-owned enterprise. To narrow down our analysis, we have decided to look at exports to the EU and at the EU anti-dumping policy as the potentially most important barrier to Chinese exports in the EU market.

The *(EU) anti-dumping policy* system has been extensively analysed in economics and law literature, but not in international business literature, see, e.g., Niels (2000). The system has generally been described as protectionistic, non-transparent, with negative welfare effects on the EU and the countries exporting to the EU.

In the international business literature *China* has been analysed to a large extent in relation to the market entry forms of foreign companies (contractual, exporting, joint venture and sole venture with 100% share of foreign ownership). Factors decisive in the choice between, e.g., a joint venture with a local Chinese partner or a wholly foreign-owned enterprise has been the primary research objective, see Gomes-Casseres (1990), Yigan Pan (1996) and Vanhonacher (1997).

This paper extensively analyses the *triangle* formed by the (EU) anti-dumping policy, China and business policy. But instead of looking at how companies can use the anti-dumping policy as a shelter (as discussed in Rugman and Verbeke (1990) and Rugman and Gestrin (1991)),[1] we consider the EU anti-dumping policy as something given, and investigate to what extent and how Chinese firms exposed to anti-dumping may be able to sustain or at least not lose too much in competitiveness on the EU market. Because Chinese companies' internationalisation until now primarily has been in exports we choose to look at the price strategies Chinese companies may use in the EU market. Following Dutta et al. (2002), the lesson we want to give to exporters from China is: "Pricing is complex. [..] The ability to set the right price at the right time, anytime, is also becoming increasingly important. [..] Once a bad price is established it can be devilish to fix."

In section two, the rules and procedures of the EU anti-dumping policy (AD) are presented. In section three, a number of empirical facts concerning the EU AD toward China will be introduced. The "non-market economy problem" and "individual treatment problem" of the EU anti-dumping policy are touched upon in section four. In section five, we present our advice how to formulate an export price strategy, and in section six, the concluding remarks of the paper will be presented.

THE EU ANTI-DUMPING POLICY:
RULES AND PROCEDURES

The EU anti-dumping regulation provides for the imposition of anti-dumping duties when the following three conditions are fulfilled: (1) There is dumping, (2) which creates material injury to the Community industry and (3) when at the same time, it is in the general interests of the Community.[2]

Dumping is present when the export price at which the product is sold in the Community market is shown to be lower than what is considered "normal value." In most cases the normal value is calculated as the price in the exporters' home market, however, a cost-based price including a profit margin is used when it is impossible to find a representative home market price.

An AD investigation is initiated by complaints from industry in the Community. The filer of the complaint hands over documentation for dumping and injury to the EU Commission. The Commission investigates the case and determines if dumping is taking place, whether or not dumped imports are causing material injury to Community industry and whether or not costs on the Community of taking measures are in proportion to the benefits. If the Council of Ministers agrees with the Commission that dumping and injury are present in the given case, the result may be a definitive measure in the form of anti-dumping duties (5 years duration, which can be extended through a so-called "expire review"). In many cases there will be no duty, but the parties will agree on price-undertakings, i.e., the exporter will increase his price in order to avoid dumping and injury.

Before 1 July 1998, all Chinese (and Russian) companies were treated as non-market economy companies.[3] In anti-dumping cases against non-market economy companies, one dumping margin calculation is typically made for the country in question ("the one country one duty rule") by comparing weighted export prices with the normal value based on information from companies in a market economy, the so-called analogue country.[4] The philosophy behind using an analogue country when calculating the normal value is due to the belief that state intervention distorts home market prices and costs making them unusable in normal value calculations.

Because of the ongoing reforms in China, which have led to an increasing number of Chinese companies operating on market economy principles, the basic regulation was changed as of 1 July 1998.[5] According to the new regulation, Chinese companies may apply for individual market economy status (MES), in which case the normal value is based on the home market price or a cost-based price of the company. The criterion that the companies have to fulfil is that there must not be any significant external interference in their economic decision-making in relation to prices, costs, investments, etc. Furthermore, the companies have to have a clear set of accounting records independently audited in line with international standards, and these must be subject to bankruptcy and property laws. Finally, their exchange rate conversions must be carried out at the market rate.[6]

For Chinese companies not applying for or getting MES, there is a possibility (which also existed before July 1998) of individual treatment, which is as an exception to the "one country one duty rule."[7] The conditions for getting individual treatment (IT) are based on the export activities of the company (freedom to determine export prices and quantities as well as their terms and conditions) and not sales conditions in the domestic situation, which are also important for getting MES. The important point is that state intervention is not so significant, that circumvention of anti-dumping measures is possible. For example, the number of state officials on the board or in key management positions should be in clear minority. If a company can prove that its export activities are determined by market forces and not affected by state influence, an individual dumping margin may be calculated based on the export prices of the company and the normal value from an analogue country. The advantage of the company getting individual treatment is that it is the export prices of that particular country that count and not the average export prices of all exporting companies in the given industry in the country. The calculated dumping margin and the imposed duty will typically be lower in the case of individual treatment. Fulfilling the criteria of MES involves individual treatment, but not the other way round.

THE EU ANTI-DUMPING POLICY AGAINST CHINA– SOME FACTS

The total number of definite EU anti-dumping measures (duties and/or undertakings) in force on 31 December 2001 was 174 (Commission, 2001a).[8] Asia was the most affected region with 114 cases, and with 34 instances China (excluding Hong Kong which had 1 case) was the individual country with the highest number. This corresponds to 20% of the total number. Given that the Chinese share of the EU's imports is 6-7% (Commission, 2001b), China is clearly overrepresented in

AD-cases. In more than 50% of the cases, Chinese products affected by EU anti-dumping measures are chemicals, coal and steel products. Furthermore, products like bicycles, lighters, footwear, handbags and a few electronic products are also affected. In general, these are low-tech products. Even though the share of Chinese exports to the EU subject to AD-measures is still at a rather low level, the real effect on Chinese export may be much larger given that the potential threat of an anti-dumping investigation may discipline Chinese exporters' price behaviour to avoid an anti-dumping investigation.

The measures used against China are primarily duties and, very infrequently, price undertakings, which more often are accepted from companies from other countries. Since 1997 no price undertakings have been used in relation to Chinese companies, whereas in the beginning of the 1990s, 21% (1991) of Chinese anti-dumping cases involved both duties and undertakings. The percentage for all countries in total concerning cases of price undertakings has also gone down, though only from 37% in 1991 to 28% in 2001 (Commission, 2001a).

Consequently, it can be stated that there is a clear tendency of increasing difficulties for Chinese companies to get price undertakings accepted. This tightening of the EU anti-dumping policy against China has gone hand in hand with China's involvement in an increasing share of all AD-cases. Furthermore it is worth paying attention to the fact that the size of the calculated dumping margins and the levels of the duties used against China are typically higher than for other countries (for the same products).

China is also overrepresented in anti-absorption and anti-circumvention investigations. A company is said to absorb a duty if it bears the cost of the duty and thereby increases the dumping margin to be able to stay in the market. To reduce the potential effect of absorption, a specific (instead of an ad valorem) duty is often used against Chinese companies. If an anti-absorption investigation is initiated, it will usually result in an increase in the tariff. In the glyphosate case,[9] the original tariff of 24% was increased to 48%, given roughly the same sales price in the European market, with the result that the Chinese exporter got a lower export price without getting more sales.[10]

Circumvention occurs when anti-dumping measures are circumvented by means of transhipment through other countries or production in other countries for which there is insufficient due cause or economic justification other than avoiding the imposition of the duty.[11] In the glyphosate case mentioned above, an anti-circumvention investigation was started in May 2001 concerning Chinese producers' transhipment through Malaysia or Taiwan or formulation glyphosate originating in China in these countries. This investigation ended by extending the tariff to imports of glyphosate consigned from Malaysia and Taiwan. This result is common in anti-circumvention cases. However, the result can also turn out like in the artificial corundum case:[12] A change from price undertakings to a definite duty because other Chinese exporters, whom the EU Commission did not earlier know, exported the product.

The fact that the EU Commission can and often does initiate anti-absorption and anti-circumvention investigations, usually on the initiative of the EU producers, shows that there is a big risk of Chinese producers either losing (anti-absorption) or at least not gaining (anti-circumvention) when attempting to use loopholes in the EU anti-dumping system.

MARKET ECONOMY STATUS
AND INDIVIDUAL TREATMENT

As mentioned above, Chinese companies have the possibility of improving the outcome of an AD investigation by applying for individual treatment (IT), or by applying for market economy status (MES) after 1 July 1998.

In the period from 1 July 1998 until 31 December 2001, 32 new AD cases were initiated, of which six were not decided before 31 December 2001, and five have been terminated due to a withdrawal of the complaint before the investigation of the Commission was completed. This leaves 21 cases for the investigation of the problem concerning market economy treatment and individual treatment. Seven of these 21 cases are so-called "expire reviews"–reviews of former cases when they are expiring. Two are "reviews of new exporters," that is current cases with definite measures, which involve new exporters who are starting their exports to the EU. Since there are possibilities for applying for MES or IT in relation to expire and new exporters reviews, these 9 cases have been included. The following analysis of MES and IT is based on an investigation of all 21 cases as published in the Official Journal of the EU Commission.[13]

Market Economy Status

In all 21 cases, at least 55 out of at least 432 Chinese producers applied for MES (13%), but only 8 companies were awarded MES! That gives a "rate of success" for MES of maximum 15%. If we exclude expire and new exporters reviews, which have another character than the new investigations, the figures are as follows: At least 52 out of at least 63 producers applied for MES (83%) and 7 received it; so the rate of "success" were 14%.[14]

MES was awarded in the compact discs boxes case, the ferromolyden case, zinc oxides case (3 companies), the integrated electronic compact fluorescent lamps case (2 companies) and the stainless fasteners case (new exporters review).

According to information from the EU Commission there were at least 6 Chinese production plants in the *compact discs boxes* case, of which 4 were wholly owned by 3 Hong Kong based companies. The 4 exporting Chinese companies applied for MES. Only two of these applications were well considered. For one of them (A) MES was refused because production was carried out in an inward processing arrangement without the permission to sell in the Chinese market and separately audited accounts. The other (Hong Kong) company (B) produced in two plants (*a* and *b*) in China, also under inward processing arrangements. However, only subsidiary *a* did fulfil the requirements for MES. It had company status in China, was subject to bankruptcy laws and independent of the state, and it also had independent audited accounts, etc. The other subsidiary (*b*) was characterised like A and not fulfilling the requirement for MES. Consequently, two subsidiaries of the same parent company in the same country can be treated quite differently with respect to getting MES status. Seen from an EU Commission point of view, intra-company differences in duties create risks of circumvention with exports going through the low duty (MES) plant. Therefore, in the compact discs boxes case, a common tariff was introduced for the two plants.

In the *integrated electronic compact fluorescent lamps* case, 10 companies applied for MES. Only Lisheng Electronic&Lighting Co. Ltd., a wholly foreign-owned company, and Phillips&Yaming Lighting Co., a joint venture with a foreign share of 60%, received MES. It is interesting that the joint venture could get MES in spite of the fact that a share of 40% of the venture belonged to the Chinese State. The argument of the Commission was that "sufficient safeguards existed which ensured that the State Company could not unduly influence the operation of the joint venture."[15]

Also, in the new exporters review of *stainless steel fasteners*, the owner structure seems important. Bulten Fastener Co. Ltd., a company wholly owned by Swedish Finnveden was awarded MES. This case also clearly illustrates the importance of getting MES or IT. If this company had not applied for MES (or IT), but instead had accepted the tariff rate for other companies (without MES or IT), the difference in the duty rate would have been 74.7 − 18.5 = 56.2 percentage point, a quite significant difference in relation to competitiveness in the European market! In the *ferromolyden* case, a private limited liability company called Nanjing Metalink got MES. The company seems to be dominated by Hong Kong "foreign" capital.[16] In the *zinc oxides* case, five companies applied for MES, but only three received it. Once more, the companies who got MES were companies with foreign capital and the refusals were based on significant state interference.[17]

The general picture we see is "not surprisingly" that foreign capital is a good basis for getting MES since foreign capital logically reduces state influence and typically involves a knowledge transfer to the Chinese company in relation to, e.g., accounting standards.[18]

However, as the *aluminium foil* case shows, a joint venture partner is not a sufficient prerequisite for getting MES. The applying Chinese company was a majority state-owned company with the chairman of the board appointed by the state. The claim of the company was that the US joint venture partner was solely responsible for the management of operations and consequently independence of the state, was not taken for granted. Therefore, it is most likely easier to convince the EU Commission that a wholly foreign-owned company operating in China is working on market economy conditions than a joint venture with a Chinese partner. Therefore, the entry mode for foreign investors whose purpose is using China as an export platform is moving towards wholly owned subsidiaries and away from equity joint ventures. Foreign investors feel frustrated with joint ventures, even though it is now easier to establish a joint venture (Deng, 2000). A wholly owned company encounters minimal resistance from authorities; it does not require a board of directors and avoids the problem of shared control (Vanhonacher, 1997).

Of the 90% refusals of MES, the general arguments have been (1) too big a state influence in relation to domestic and export sales, and also staffing, and (2) insufficient accounting systems. Seen from the perspective of an all-Chinese company wanting to export to the EU, the two problems will be reduced by entering into a joint venture with a foreign company, which does not have too low a share of foreign capital and with foreigners in the leading managers and board positions. Furthermore, it is important to get the right to sell in the domestic Chinese market as well as getting an export license.

Individual Treatment

After July 1998, the success rate of an application for individual treatment (excluding those companies that were given MES) is 58%, a number that has been increasing with time. The number of applications in relation to the number of potential applicants is very high when disregarding expire- and new exporters reviews. The low number of applicants in the reviews is presumably due to the fact that if a company has been refused in one investigation, its motivation for trying again is fairly low, unless the company has undergone big changes in relation to its freedom of exporting. The relatively high refusal rate (42%) is explained by the fear of circumvention by channelling exports through the exporter with the lowest duty rate, when exporters are not independent. Prior to 1990 the EU did not determine any individual export prices for China's exporters meaning that no individual treatment was given, following the principle of "one country one duty." Consequently, even though the number of IT relative to the potential number is less than 6%, the increase in this number over time could be an indication of a development towards a less controlled export system in China.

The owner structure of the companies is also important in IT investigations. In the *hairbrushes* case, MES was not awarded to 3 applicants, but IT was given to all 7 applicants. An important factor behind the refusals of MES was that the companies were not allowed to sell on the Chinese market. However, this factor is of no great importance in relation to getting the IT, which primarily depends on the freedom in export behaviour. Furthermore, since all 7 companies were wholly or predominantly foreign-owned, the state influence in exports and risks of circumvention were minimal.

Generally, co-operation (inclusive complete answers to the Commission's questionnaires) is important. In the *malleable cast iron tube or pipe fittings* case, one applicant for IT was refused even though "it was eligible for individual treatment, but the questionnaire reply was incomplete regarding reporting of export sales."

FORMULATION OF A PRICE STRATEGY

It is now possible to formulate a number of propositions for managers in companies in China, which have been subject to or may be subject to an anti-dumping investigation in the future. The *Figure 1* gives an over-

FIGURE 1. How to Formulate a Price Strategy

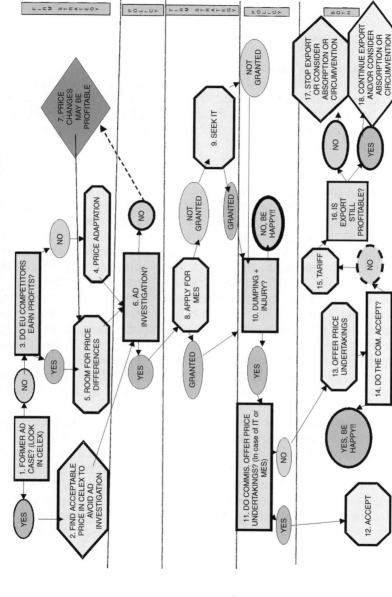

Note: In each part of the figure separated by the horizontal lines decision-making is done at the firm level, the EU-policy level or both.

135

view over the necessary steps in formulation of a price strategy for the EU market.

In order to prevent being subject to an EU anti-dumping investigation, the export price of the Chinese company in the EU market is an important factor. It is important for the Chinese company to discover if there have been former anti-dumping cases against Chinese producers or producers from other countries for the given product. This can very easily be verified by using the database CELEX (1).[19,20] If such an investigation proves that there has been a former anti-dumping case, there is a big risk that a new one will be commenced, if the price of the Chinese company is not close to the existing level in the EU market (perhaps corrected for quality differences). The information in CELEX concerning former anti-dumping investigations will give an indication of an "acceptable" export price level (2). If there has not been anti-dumping investigations for the given product type earlier, the Chinese company should be very careful about its analysis of European competitors. Experience has shown that if competitors are doing well in relation to actual performance, the risk of an anti-dumping investigation is small compared to the situation where they are performing badly, e.g., because of the business cycle or structural changes (losing comparative advantages) (OECD, 2000; Mah, 2000) (3). So the general lesson is not to deviate too much in prices from the European competitors (with the obvious consequence that sales will shrink). Therefore, the Chinese company is faced with a choice between accommodation of prices in order to avoid an AD investigation (and the risk of duties) (4), and no price adaptation with the hope of not being "detected" by the competitors (5).[21]

If an investigation has been initiated (6), it is important for the given company to try to acquire market economy treatment because, in this way, the calculation of dumping margins are based on the conditions of the firm and therefore less arbitrary (8).[22] According to experience (from Russian, Ukrainian and Chinese cases), tariffs and price undertakings will be more favourable. The main condition is to be independent of the state or the local government in relation to price fixing, wage policy, the right both to export and sell in the Chinese market and putting together the board of the company. Besides that, it is important to use international accounting standards. A joint venture with an international company is not a sufficient condition to acquire MES, but it certainly does increase the probability. For wholly foreign-owned companies, the probability is further enhanced. For Chinese companies wanting to enter the world market, the process of becoming independent of the state and getting a non-Chinese joint venture partner should be started as early as possible. Especially fulfilling the criteria of accounting standards seems very easy when one enters into a joint venture with a foreign partner.

If an anti-dumping investigation is not opened (after a given period of time) it could be perceived by the Chinese company as an indication that its export prices in the EU market have not provoked the European competitors and for that reason export prices may be somewhat reduced (7).

If MES cannot be acquired, it is important to try to acquire individual treatment in relation to dumping margins and tariffs/price undertakings, since individual treatment (like MES) typically results in less severe measures (9).[23] Besides some of the conditions for acquiring MES (e.g., independence of the state), it is generally a question of willingness to co-operate with the EU Commission in relation to providing relevant information. "If an interested party does not co-operate, or co-operates only partially, so that relevant information is thereby withheld, the result may be less favourable to the party than if it had co-operated."[24]

If a provisional or final determination of dumping and injury caused by such dumping has been made (10), there is a possibility that the Commission will offer the company an agreement to increase export prices (price undertakings) (11). In such a case, the company should gladly accept the offer because the alternative to pay tariffs is worse (12). In the case that the Commission does not offer price undertakings, the Chinese company should take the initiative to give the EU Commission an offer to raise the export prices, but it must also know that there are rather tight deadlines to follow[25] (13). If this is accepted (14), the company will avoid paying tariffs for the next five years at least and it can cash the tariff revenue as "profits." However, as already mentioned the practice of the EU Commission since 1997 has been not to offer price undertakings to Chinese companies. But in line with the Chinese membership of the WTO and the expected increase in attainment of MES, it is not unreasonable that price undertakings will be given to Chinese companies in the future.

If negotiations on price undertakings do not give any result, a tariff will be imposed on the company (15) with the potential consequence that exports no longer are profitable because of too little sales, given an unchanged export price (16). In a situation like that, the Chinese company may either stop exports or try to keep a considerable share of the European market through export price reductions or keeping export prices unchanged trying to avoid the tariff by exporting through a country without anti-dumping tariffs. For both the absorption and circumvention strategy, there is a big risk of detection, which may result in a higher level of tariff, consequently stopping export (17).

If exports are still profitable after the tariff, a continuation of exports seems natural, but absorption and circumvention may still be a hazardous possibility to improve export profitability (18).

A *new* exporter in the EU market in products, where AD-measures are in force, should not necessarily accept the existing duties. Through a special effort in a new exporters review, there are possibilities of getting other conditions than those prevailing. This is also the case in expire reviews, where the investigation is based on the "old" method (for non-market economy companies), but the company can ask for a parallel MES investigation.

If the Chinese company feels that it has received an unfair treatment by the EU AD-system, it has a number of possibilities for complaining. First of all to the Commission, but if that proves unsuccessful, the company can complain to the EU Court of Justice. Generally, using Brussels based lawyers specialising in EU anti-dumping legislation is considered a good idea. The Chinese membership of the WTO gives Chinese companies an opportunity to check the legality of the EU anti-dumping decisions by using the dispute settlement system of the WTO.

However, the Chinese membership of the WTO will also change the rules of the anti-dumping game against China for other reasons. If Chinese producers who are under investigation by the Commission can *clearly* show that market economy conditions prevail in the industry that produces a similar product with regards to the manufacturing, production and sale of the product, the EU shall use Chinese prices or costs (WTO, 2001). Now, the Chinese producers have a WTO legal right to get MES if market economy conditions are obvious instead of just having the possibility of applying for MES and waiting for the approval or rejection. In any event, the possibility of using a method for calculating the normal value that is not based on market economy principles shall expire 15 years after the date of Chinese accession (WTO, 2001).

Other, more indirect, parts of the Chinese accession conditions may also influence the use of MES and IT in the coming years. Within three years after accession, all enterprises in China shall have the right to trade in all goods, including the right to import and export. Along with elimination of price control, this is the main condition for getting IT and also an important factor behind getting MES. Furthermore, living up to the WTO requirements could be considered complementary to the Chinese reform process, with a gradual reduction of the influence of central authorities on the management of non-privatised companies.

CONCLUSION

This paper has shown that EU anti-dumping policy has been extensively applied, both in relation to the number and size of measures, especially to companies operating with China as their production base.

This paper also shows that companies operating in China, exporting to or planning to export to the EU market, have a number of possibilities for lessening the threat of or the size of EU anti-dumping measures. Firstly, the companies have to use the information given by the EU institutions in relation to AD-cases. This information can be useful for Chinese companies in formulating their price strategies on the EU market. Secondly, since the treatment of a Chinese company depends on the strength of its linkages to Chinese public authorities, dependency should be reduced. There are numerous possibilities for this. A state-owned Chinese company could try to be privatised or enter into a joint venture with a foreign company making sure that the joint venture gets an export license and the right to sell on the Chinese domestic market. Combined with an application of getting market economy status or at least individual treatment, the possibilities for a lower level of duty are present. By entering into negotiations with the EU, the Chinese company may also have the possibility of getting a permission to convert a duty into a price undertaking resulting in better economic performance. For a foreign company investing in China our cases have shown that the company should prefer a wholly owned company or at least acquire the majority ownership. This result is in accordance with the literature on entry modes in China, saying that to protect its ownership advantage the company should prefer a wholly owned company or a majority stake in a joint venture. Our study thus adds to the literature by stressing how the optimal entry mode for foreign companies in China may also be influenced by the anti-dumping policy of the surrounding world.

The overall conclusion is rather paradoxical, however. Often it does not pay for a Chinese company trying to enter the EU market to deviate too much in its export price from the present EU price level, because the result can easily be an AD investigation, leading to tariffs or price undertakings, which will neutralise the low prices. But if this advice is followed, the company will find it very difficult to enter the EU market because the consumers and the user industry often will not prefer "identically" priced Chinese products, given the low perceived quality, as stated in the literature on the "country of origin effects," see, e.g., Wyang and Lamb (1983).

Since the conclusion of the Uruguay Round and the founding of the WTO, anti-dumping laws have become much more important. Now 120 countries have these laws at their disposal, including China. There is no doubt that anti-dumping laws will become the most important types of protectionism as traditional tariffs and quotas fade away. Since it is unlikely that the anti-dumping laws will be repealed in the near future, it seems obvious that companies in China should learn how to behave in international markets characterised by extensive use of anti-dumping, especially because these firms are supposed to continue being the main target for anti-dumping actions. Hopefully, this paper will add to the learning process of Chinese companies.

The conclusions above are based on the "average" historical experiences of the EU anti-dumping policy against China in 1990-2001. Consequently, they do not necessarily apply to every industry or in the future. Furthermore, the analysis is based solely on information from the EU Commission, which may bias the results. Further research might attempt to reduce this problem by sending questionnaires to Chinese exporters to gather information on their views of the EU anti-dumping policy, including to the extent to which this policy has influenced or will influence their price policy in the EU market and their choice of ownership structure.

NOTES

1. Czinkota and Kotae (1997) empirically investigated how large firms in the U.S. can use the anti-dumping process to obtain strategic shelter from foreign competitors even under conditions of growing markets, while smaller firms in more atomistic industries are likely to gain such shelter only in instances of market decline. Furthermore, Marsh (1998) has shown how anti-dumping statues are effective in improving the performance of U.S. firms, suggesting that the anti-dumping laws significantly increase returns to U.S. firms that pursue anti-dumping protection.

2. The current Community anti-dumping legislation ("Basic Regulation") is Council Regulation (EC) No 3847/96 of 22 December 1995 (OJ L 56, 6.3.1996) as last amended by Regulation (EC) No 905/98 (OJ L 128, 30.04.1998) and Commission Decision No 2277/96/ECSC of 28.11.1996 (OJ L 308, 29.11.1996).

3. In AD investigations the People's Republic of China (in the following just "China") and Hong Kong are treated as two countries; Hong Kong as a market economy and China as a non-market economy, where companies can apply for market economy status in the latter.

4. The GATT/WTO rule on anti-dumping for non-market economies gives the contracting parties freedom to determine normal value. In article 9 of the EU Basic Regulation it is stated, that as a general rule the "one country one duty" principle shall be used for non-market economy companies (Wang, 1999).

5. Council Regulation (EC) No 905/98 (OJ L 128, 30.04.1998).

6. China accepted as a Member of the International Monetary Fund full convertibility for transactions under the current account in 1995. The Chinese currency is not yet convertible for capital account transactions (Houben, 1999).

7. Dumping companies in market economies are typically treated individually, unless it is impossible (because of lack of co-operation) or impractical (many exporters). In their anti-dumping practice prior to 1990 the EU did not determine any individual export prices for Chinese exporters (Wang, 1999). There were isolated cases in the early 1990s, but this development experienced a set-back in 1993 with the Chinese bicycle case (Commission Regulation (EEC) No. 550/93 of March 1993). Since 1996, however, the individual treatment policy has experienced a "renaissance" (Rydelski, 1998).

8. A case is defined as one product plus one country, independent of the measure, duty, price undertakings or a combination of two of these factors. The total number is counted at 31st December.

9. Official Journal L 124, 25/05/2000.

10. Seen from a purely welfare economic point of view the Chinese companies absorption of duties are beneficial to the EU. This argument is parallel to the optimal tariff argumentation for big countries imposing tariffs.

11. See article 13 in Council Regulation, OJ L056, 06/03/1996.

12. See Council Regulation, OJ L276, 09/10/97.

13. Aluminium foil (OJ L134, 17/05/2001); Coke of coal in pieces with a diameter of more than 80 mm (OJ L316, 15/12/2000); Electronic weighing scales (OJ L301, 30/11/2000); Glycine (OJ L118, 19/05/2000); Hairbrushes (OJ L111, 09/05/2000); Cathode-ray colour television picture tubes (OJ L267, 20/10/2000); Stainless steel fasteners and parts thereof (OJ L297, 24/11/2000); Bicycles (OJ L175, 14/07/2000); Silicon carbide (OJ L125, 26/05/2000); Deadburned magnesia (OJ L46, 18/02/2000); Handbags, leather (OJ L22, 27/01/2000); Ferrosilicon (OJ L84, 23/03/2001); Gas-fuelled, non-refillable flint lighters and refillable pocket flint lighters (OJ L248, 18/09/2001); Potassium permanganate (OJ L44, 15/02/2001); Malleable cast iron tube or pipe fittings (OJ L208, 18/08/2000); Hot-rolled flat products of non-alloy steel (OJ L202, 10/08/2000); Compact discs boxes (OJ L310, 04/12/1999); Ferromolyden (OJ L214, 08/08/2001); Fluorspar (OJ L241, 26/09/2000); Zinc oxides (OJ L62, 05/03/2002); Integrated electronic compact fluorescent lamps (OJ L195, 19/07/2001).

14. The lack of exactness in relation to number of producers is due to the imprecise information given by the Commission in its Regulations.

15. Official Journal L195, 19/07/2001.

16. This statement is based on a not very precise information given by the Metalink to the author.

17. The three companies who got MES were: (1) Liuzhou Nonferrous Metals Smelting Co. Ltd–100% owned by a Canadian investor (information to the author from the company); (2) Liuzhou Fuxin Chemical Industry Co. Ltd–the ownerstructure is unknown and (3) Gredman Guingang Chemical Ltd.–who is located in Batang Maijiupo–a development zone for Enterprises with foreign Investment.

18. That MES is beneficial to a company is confirmed by a Commission statement in relation to recognition of Russia as "Market Economy" May 2002. In this statement it is said "Russia will crucially be able to benefit from the accompanying treatment in anti-dumping cases, an issue of key interest to both the Russian authorities and busi-

ness community (*http://europa.eu.int.comm*/external_relations/russia/summit_05_02/ ip02_775.htm).

19. CELEX is the most reliable and widely known information source on European Community law. It was launched on the web in 1997. It includes most acts published in the L and C series of the Official Journal of the European Communities (OJ) within days of their publication.

20. The numbers (1), (2), etc., used in the following refer to the numbers used in Figure 1.

21. In some cases it may be an advantage for a company operating in China that an AD investigation is started! For a MES company (be it a wholly foreign-owned, a joint venture with foreign capital or a wholly Chinese private-owned company) an AD investigation ending with duties can function as means to weaken the competitiveness of local state-owned or state subsidised companies within the given industry. That could have been the case in the integrated electronic compact fluorescent lamps case, where the complainants are the European Lighting Companies Federation representing major proportion of EU production, including Phillips Lighting B.V. So Phillips is both an initiator of an AD investigation and influenced through its Chinese joint venture. Phillips withdrew from the complaint after the initiation of the proceeding and stopped manufacturing of the product in the EU shortly after!

22. The definition of the dumping margin (DM) is: $DM = PN - PX$, with PN the normal value and PX the export price. If the company gets MES, it can influence both PN and PX and therefore it has a greater autonomy in relation to avoid dumping accusations. If it cannot get MES it can only influence PX, and in principle whatever PX it chooses, there can be dumping because selection of the analogue country is to a large extent the free choice of the EU institutions and therefore subject to lobby activities of the complainant industry.

23. The integrated electronic compact fluorescent lamps case shows that a MES company may get a higher duty than a non-MES company who gets IT.

24. Article 18 in Council regulation, OJ L056, 06/03/1996.

25. Article 8 in Council regulation, OJ L056, 06/03/1996.

REFERENCES

Chih-Kang, W., & Lamb Jr, C. (1983). The impact of selected environmental forces upon consumers' willingness to buy foreign products. *Journal of the Academy of Marketing Science*, 11, 71-84.

Commission of European Communities (2001a). *Anti-dumping. Anti-subsidy. Statistics covering the year 2001.* Available at: *http://europa.eu.int/comm/trade/policy/dumping/reports.htm*

Commission of the European Communities (2001b). Available at: *http://europa.eu.int/comm/trade/wto_overview/stat.htm*

Czinkota, M. R. & Kotabe, M. (1997). A marketing perspective of the U.S. international trade commission's antidumping actions–An empirical inquiry. *Journal of World Business*, 32(2), 169-187.

Deng, P. (2001). WFOEs: The most popular entry mode into China. *Business Horizons*, July-August, 63-72.

Dutta, S., Bergen, M., Levy, D., Ritson, M. & Zbaracki, M. (2002). Pricing as a strategic capability. *MIT Sloan Management Review*, 43(3), 61-66.

Gomes-Casseres, B. (1990). Firm ownership preferences and host government restrictions: An integrated approach. *Journal of International Business Studies*, 21(1), 1-22.

Houben, H. (1999). China's economic reforms and integration into the World trading system. *Journal of World Trade*, 33(3), 1-18.

Mah, J. S. (2000). Antidumping decisions and macroeconomic variables in the USA. *Applied Economics*, 32, 1701-1709.

Marsh, S. J. (1998). Creating barriers for foreign competitors: A study of the impact of anti-dumping actions on the performance of U.S. Firms. *Strategic Management Journal*, 19, 25-37.

Niels, G. (2000). What is antidumping really about. *Journal of Economic Surveys*, 1(4), 467-492.

OECD. (2000). *The European Union's trade policies and their economic effects*. OECD, Paris.

Pan, Y. (1994). Influences on foreign equity ownership level in joint ventures in China. *Journal of International Business Studies*, 27(1), 1-26.

Pauwels, W., Vandenbussche, H. & Weverbergh, M. (2001). Strategic behaviour under European antidumping duties. *International Journal of Economics of Business*, 8(1), 75-99.

Rugman, A. & Verbeke, A. (1990). *Global strategy and trade policy*. Croom Helm/ Routledge, London and New York.

Rugman, A. & Gestrin, M. (1991). US trade laws as barriers to globalization. Paper presented at the Fourth IBEAR research conference on "The globalization of American firms" at the University of Southern California. Los Angeles, 20-21 June.

Rydelski, M. S. (1998). The Community's new anti-dumping practice towards China and Russia. *Europäische Zeitschrift für Wirtschaftsrecht*, 19, 586-589.

Vanhonacker, W. (1997). Entering China: An unconventional approach. *Harvard Business Review*, 75(2), 130-137.

Wang, J. (1999). A critique of the application to China of the non-market economy rules of anti-dumping legislation and practice of the European Union. *Journal of World Trade*, 33, 117-145.

World Trade Organisation (2001). Accession of the People's Republic of China. Decision of 10 November 2001. Available at: *http://docsonline.wto.org/imrd/*

Impact of Fear Appeals
in a Cross-Cultural Context

Anne-Marie Vincent
Alan J. Dubinsky

SUMMARY. The purpose of the present study was to examine the influence of culture on fear, using the protection motivation model as a basic theoretical framework. A 2×2 between-subjects experiment was conducted in the United States and in France. Participants were first shown a high threat or low threat advertisement. They were then asked to complete a questionnaire designed to measure fear, maladaptive coping, and purchase intention. A two-way multivariate analysis of covariance was used to test the hypotheses.

Results indicated that compared to a low level of threat, a high level induces greater fear and leads to a higher likelihood of purchasing the advertised product. However, no significant differences on fear were found between French and U.S. subjects. Exploratory findings suggest that adaptive, instead of maladaptive, coping could play a mediating role

---

Anne-Marie Vincent is Market Research Analyst, Center for Public Opinion Research, Inc., Montreal, Canada. Alan J. Dubinsky is Professor, School of Consumer and Family Sciences, 1262 Matthews Hall, West Lafayette, IN 47907-1262 (E-mail: dubinsky@purdue.edu).

Address correspondence to: Alan J. Dubinsky, Professor, School of Consumer and Family Sciences, 1262 Matthews Hall, West Lafayette, IN 47907-1262 (E-mail: dubinsky@purdue.edu).

[Haworth co-indexing entry note]: "Impact of Fear Appeals in a Cross-Cultural Context." Vincent, Anne-Marie, and Alan J. Dubinsky. Co-published simultaneously in *Journal of Euromarketing* (International Business Press, an imprint of The Haworth Press, Inc.) Vol. 14, No. 1/2, 2004, pp. 145-167; and: *Marketing Issues in Western Europe: Changes and Developments* (eds: Erdener Kaynak, and Frédéric Jallat) International Business Press, an imprint of The Haworth Press, Inc., 2004, pp. 145-167. Single or multiple copies of this article are available for a fee from The Haworth Document Delivery Service [1-800-HAWORTH, 9:00 a.m. - 5:00 p.m. (EST). E-mail address: docdelivery@haworthpress.com].

between fear and purchase intention. The theoretical and managerial implications of the findings are discussed, and suggestions regarding the design of future fear appeals studies are provided. *[Article copies available for a fee from The Haworth Document Delivery Service: 1-800-HAWORTH. E-mail address: <docdelivery@haworthpress.com> Website: <http://www.HaworthPress.com> © 2004 by The Haworth Press, Inc. All rights reserved.]*

KEYWORDS. Fear appeals, advertising, consumer behavior, France, cross-cultural management, uncertainty avoidance

Ferment in health, political, social, economic, technological, and environmental arenas today presents an array of serious issues. For instance, pestilences (such as AIDS) are a bane in numerous developing countries. Right-wing political parties have become increasingly popular in parts of Europe and elsewhere, raising concerns about the potential for declining civil liberties in those nations. Many metropolitan areas the world-over are becoming increasingly overpopulated, thus straining local government budgets and infrastructures. Financial shocks are widespread, as the erstwhile economic good times have given way to fiscal failures, as well as recessionary and even deflationary pressures. Cloning and biotechnology raise the specter of Frankenstein-like entities if such scientific opportunities are misused. And global warming, oil tanker spills, and excessive pollution have contributed to degradation of human and non-human ecosystems.

Arguably, then, today's dynamism fosters myriad fear-inducing threats that are real, that are upon us, and that have dramatic influence. Fear is a frequently experienced phenomenon of individuals and can arise in the face of major or minor circumstances. Aware of this, some advertisers utilize communications designed to cause fear in the target audience, which hopefully will lead individuals to respond in the manner desired by the advertisers. Rather than emphasizing the benefits of using a product or service, fear appeals "inform consumers of the risks of using a product or of not using one" (Assael 1995, p. 728).

Emotional appeals play an important role in persuasion. In fact, a persuasive message has been found to be more likely to lead to attitude change if the receiver is emotionally aroused rather than if he/she is exposed to a more rational communication (Arnold 1985). Extant work investigating the effect of emotion-arousing messages has concentrated its efforts on fear appeals that have been shown to lead people to engage in salutary behaviors (Breckler 1993). In fact, fear is widely used in persuasive communications to promote healthy behaviors and to develop social awareness concerning such issues as road safety or environmental issues (Girandola 2000). And advertisements portraying fear lead to better recall than more cheerful ads or messages with no emotional content (LaTour, Snipes, and Bliss 1996).

The use of fear appeals in persuasive messages has been extensively researched in the past five decades, and numerous models have been presented to explain the process. Fear appeal models, however, have been chiefly developed by Western scholars and tested in Western-based samples. Maheswaran and Shavitt (2000) stress the importance of validating theoretical frameworks in other cultures in order to increase their robustness. Indeed, Lavack (1997) has called for a need to examine the effectiveness of fear appeals across different cultures. Investigations of fear appeals in cross-cultural situations, though, are virtually nonexistent.

Past research in cross-cultural advertising has focused mainly on one facet of cultural variation, individualism-collectivism. But Maheswaran and Shavitt (2000) argue that other dimensions of cultural variability also deserve attention. One is uncertainty avoidance. *Uncertainty avoidance* has been conceptualized as the extent to which a culture is anxious about uncertain situations and therefore establishes structure to avoid experiencing this continuous threat (Hofstede 1980). The dimension of uncertainty avoidance seems particularly relevant to the study of fear appeals owing to its association with an increased need for security.

An understanding of cultural differences is essential to communicate effectively to consumers from different cultural backgrounds. In the present study, France and the United States were chosen as target countries to represent opposite ends of the uncertainty avoidance continuum. Because these two Western countries share similar political, social, economic, and value systems (Biswas, Olsen, and Carlet 1992), though, marketers may incorrectly perceive them as comparable, which could ultimately lead to ineffective advertising campaigns.

The aforementioned limitations of prior work on the impact of fear appeals in advertising led to the present investigation. The objectives of this study are two-fold: (1) to examine the impact of the level of fear on consumer responses; and (2) to assess whether culture is an antecedent of fear in the persuasive process. The balance of the paper reviews germane literature and develops hypotheses, describes the method, reports the results, and offers implications.

LITERATURE REVIEW

The effects of fear arousal on attitude change have been debated extensively over the past 40 years. The first study on this issue concluded that a *low level* of fear arousal induced more conformity to the recommendations in the message since high fear arousal communications increased defensiveness and produced resistance to persuasion (Janis and Fesbach 1953). Some subsequent studies confirmed this negative relationship (Janis and Terwilliger 1962), while others argued for a curvilinear relationship, where moderate levels of fear arousal are more effective than low or high (Janis 1967; Janis and Leventhal 1968). Most studies, however, have indicated that increases in the level of fear arousal are generally associated with greater persuasion (for reviews, see Boster and Mongeau 1984, Sutton 1982).

A Model of Fear

In order to determine the effectiveness of fear appeals across cultures, a model of the antecedents and consequences of fear is proposed in Figure 1. The model is derived from the work of Rogers (1983) and Tanner, Hunt, and Eppright (1991), where the central role of fear is recognized, and bears resemblance to the work of Schoenbachler and Whittler (1996) (which examined teenagers' reactions to fear appeals in drug prevention public service announcements). In accordance with Rogers' reasoning, Tanner et al. (1991) argue that high fear is *evoked* when threat appraisal is high (i.e., when severity of the threat and probability of occurrence are perceived to be high). Fear is also predicted to be a mediator between the level of threat (i.e., threat appraisal) and coping response (i.e., coping appraisal process).

The level of threat is predicted to influence the level of fear aroused. In fact, research has found that the higher the severity of the threat and the higher the probability of occurrence, the greater the fear experienced (Tanner, Hunt, and Eppright 1991). Fear is assumed to affect the extent

FIGURE 1. Proposed Model for the Study

to which certain coping responses are adopted, which in turn influences behavioral intention. Coping response refers to the cognitive process where the individual generates thoughts about dealing with the reality of the threat (or not dealing with it).

Rational problem solving is the possible adaptive strategy in response to a threat and is defined as seeking information about the preventive behavior and making plans to remedy the problem (McCrae 1984). A threat can cause an individual to engage in either adaptive or maladaptive coping responses. Adaptive coping refers to having thoughts about how to deal with the fear and overcome the threat effectively. Prior empirical work, though, has determined that adaptive coping is not directly elicited by fear. In other words, past findings indicate that fear does *not* influence the development of an adaptive cognitive response; rather, it affects the likelihood of considering a maladaptive coping response (Ho 2000).

In the present context, maladaptive coping will refer to thoughts about not directly managing the threat but instead resorting to defense mechanisms such as avoidance, fatalism, or wishful thinking to handle the situation. Avoidance is related to the denial of the threat, whereas fatalism refers to the acceptance of a stressful event as unchangeable because the individual feels that nothing can be done anyway. On the other hand, wishful thinking is described as the reliance on unrealistic solutions, such as hoping for a miracle. Furthermore, previous studies on fear appeals have suggested that hopelessness is also a reaction manifested by some individuals when exposed to a threatening message (Higbee 1969, Rogers 1983). Defense mechanisms can be perceived as adaptive from a psychological perspective, since they are known to reduce distress (Rippetoe and Rogers 1987). Such coping responses, though, tend to be seen as maladaptive in the context of health promotion and disease prevention, as they represent a threat to physical well-being.

A recent study (Ho 2000) observed that fear and coping mediate the relationship between level of threat and behavioral intention. More specifically, the emotion of fear is triggered by the perceived severity of the threat and the perceived vulnerability (likelihood of occurrence). Consequently, the more severe the threat is perceived to be and the more vulnerable a person feels to that threat, the higher the fear experienced by that individual. Subsequently, the greater the fear experienced, the less likely a person is to display maladaptive coping. This might be explained by the fact that a fearful individual will realize that maladaptive thoughts will not be effective in overcoming the threat.

Hence, fear is predicted to be negatively related to maladaptive coping, which will then affect one's intention to perform the behavior recommended in the persuasive message. The lower the maladaptive coping, the more likely the individual will follow the recommendations. In essence, the higher the fear, the lower the maladaptive coping, and the higher the intention to purchase the product advertised to reduce the threat. Studies using Tanner, Hunt, and Eppright's (1991) model have only focused on messages designed to convince individuals to adopt protective-health *behaviors* (Ho 2000, Lavack 1997, Schoenbachler and Whittler 1996). The present investigation will build on past research by applying the model in an advertising context where the goal is to persuade the consumer to buy a specific *product*.

The foregoing discussion leads to the following hypotheses:

H_1:   Compared to a low level of threat, a high level of threat will induce a higher level of fear.

H_2:   The higher the level of fear, the lower the maladaptive coping.

H_3:   As maladaptive coping decreases, purchase intention for the advertised product increases.

Cultural Differences in Uncertainty Avoidance

Hofstede conducted a survey about the values of employees and managers from different national subsidiaries of IBM Corporation in 53 countries (Hofstede 1980). Four distinct dimensions emerged that discriminated across cultures: individualism-collectivism, power distance, masculinity-femininity, and uncertainty avoidance. A fifth factor, long-term/short-term orientation, was added later when a different questionnaire was developed by Chinese scholars (Chinese Culture Connection 1987). In the context of the present study, uncertainty avoidance is the sole dimension considered because it is particularly relevant to the study of fear appeals; the remaining four are not especially pertinent to fear appeals.

According to Hofstede (1991, p. 113), uncertainty avoidance is defined as "the extent to which the members of a culture feel threatened by uncertain or unknown situations." Individuals within the culture try to avoid those situations by establishing rules and rituals to control social behaviors to ensure that the continuous threat of unpredictability is somewhat overcome. As such, people living in high uncertainty avoidance countries are expected to experience less fear. Members of high uncertainty avoidance cultures, such as France, are less likely than their counterparts (such as the United States) to take risks and to accept deviant behavior and dissent (Lustig and Koester 1998). Moreover, they are more resistant to innovation, rely more on expert knowledge, and tend to be more worried about the future. On the other hand, members of low uncertainty avoidance countries define achievement more in terms of recognition than security and are less fearful of failure (Hofstede 1980).

In addition, high uncertainty avoidance cultures are characterized by higher levels of anxiety and stress. In fact, a strong positive correlation has been found between a country's uncertainty avoidance score in the IBM studies and Lynn's (1975) country anxiety scores. Lynn studied country-level medical and other related statistics to compute an anxiety score for 18 different countries. In a high uncertainty avoidance culture, anxiety is released through the expression of aggressiveness and other emotions, which is socially acceptable in these cultures (Hofstede 1991).

Uncertainty Avoidance and Fear

Izard (1971) conducted a study to examine the attitudes toward emotions in seven different countries. At the time, no interpretation of the findings had been advanced. Years later, Gudykunst and Ting-Toomey (1988) analyzed Izard's (1971) data using Hofstede's (1980) dimensions of cross-cultural variability. The results revealed that uncertainty avoidance was negatively correlated to dreading fear. According to Gudykunst and Ting-Toomey (1988), the acceptance of aggressive behavior in high uncertainty avoidance cultures might constitute an explanation of why fear is experienced to a lesser degree in such cultures.

Furthermore, Wallbott and Scherer (1986) studied antecedents of emotions across cultures. Their analysis revealed that novel situations constituted an antecedent of fear for respondents from a low uncertainty avoidance country but not for those from a high uncertainty avoidance culture. The rationale underlying this result is that in high uncertainty avoidance cultures, formal rules for interaction are developed, thus novel situations should not arouse fear. Likewise, because such cultures have institutions and structures to deal with fear, people "may tend not to recognize this emotion [fear], or attenuate attributions of intensity when expressed or perceived" (Matsumoto 1989, p. 95). Schimmack (1996) conducted a study in which judges from different cultures were asked to recognize facial expressions of emotions. The results indicated that judges from cultures high on uncertainty avoidance were less accurate in their recognition of fear, which tends to lend support to Matsumoto's (1989) assertion.

Thus, high uncertainty avoidance cultures have developed mechanisms to prevent anxiety that can be evoked in the presence of unexpected events. As such, fear is experienced at a lower degree. As noted earlier, the lower the level of fear, the higher the likelihood to produce maladaptive cognitive responses. Therefore, because members of high uncertainty avoidance cultures experience fear with less intensity than those of low uncertainty avoidance cultures, they should be more likely to generate a maladaptive coping response. Based on the previous arguments, the following hypotheses are posited:

H_4: At a high level of threat, individuals from a high uncertainty avoidance culture will report lower levels of fear than individuals from a low uncertainty avoidance culture.

H_5: At a high level of threat, members of high uncertainty avoidance cultures will exhibit more maladaptive coping than members of low uncertainty avoidance cultures.

METHOD

In order to test the hypotheses, an experiment was conducted in the United States and in France. Male and female college students from both countries were exposed to an advertisement intended to arouse either a low or high level of fear. Their coping responses to the threat were measured along with their intention to buy the advertised product.

Subjects

According to Hofstede's (1980) findings, the United States is considered a relatively low uncertainty avoidance culture, whereas France is relatively high on this dimension. Therefore, these two cultures were chosen to examine the impact of uncertainty avoidance on the effectiveness of fear appeals.

In the context of this study, participants had to be similar in terms of background characteristics in order to make valid cross-cultural comparisons. Van de Vijver and Leung (1997) note that college students from different cultures are often used in cross-cultural studies because they seemingly possess similar background characteristics. Consequently, participants in this investigation consisted of college students from two universities–one in France and a large Midwestern university in the United States. A total of 200 (100 U.S. and 100 French) students were recruited as a convenience sample at the exit of a classroom after dismissal of the class. Out of the 200 questionnaires, six were discarded when data from an entire scale were missing or if the nationality of the respondent was neither American nor French.

A total of 194 students, 101 Americans and 93 French, constituted the sample for the analyses. Statistical tests were conducted to determine whether any differences existed between gender, school year, age, and father's occupation in the French and U.S. subsamples. Significant differences were found for sex, school year, and age. So, these variables were ultimately treated as covariates.

Experimental Design

A 2×2 factorial design was used to determine the effects of two between-subjects variables on fear, maladaptive coping response, and purchase intention (dependent variables). The independent variable was threat appeal (high vs. low). Culture (France vs. United States) was a blocking variable. Subjects were assigned to a block according to their culture and were randomly assigned to a low-threat or high-threat treatment.

Procedure

The study was presented to participants as an effort to develop an advertisement for a new sunscreen. They were then exposed to either a low or high threat print advertisement. Results from a pre-test indicated that the high and low threat ads were credible and that college students from both countries were not familiar with the advertised brand. Sunscreen was selected as the focal product owing to the results of the pre-test, its protective qualities (i.e., potential for mitigating fear), and its common use among the target population (college-aged students).

After exposure to the ad, participants completed a questionnaire containing measures of fear, coping responses, and purchase intention, as well as scales of variables known to influence the intensity of the relationship between fear and purchase intention (i.e., sensation-seeking, self-esteem, and product usage). Moreover, a manipulation check of the high versus low threat was included in the questionnaire. Also, subjects provided demographic information about their age, gender, nationality, year in school, and father's occupation. At the conclusion of the experiment, subjects were debriefed and the researcher corrected any false information about the disease that was presented in the advertisement.

The questionnaire was translated into French using the translation-backtranslation method. This technique consists of translating items in another language and then backtranslating them into the original language by a different translator (Van de Vijver and Leug 1997).

Variables

One independent variable was manipulated in the experiment: threat appeal (high vs. low), while culture served as a blocking variable. The dependent variables included in this study were fear, coping response, and purchase intention.

Independent Variable. Consistent with protection motivation theory (Rogers 1983), threat level was manipulated according to the *severity* of the threat and the *probability of occurrence* of the threat perceived by the participant. The manipulation was adapted from Rippetoe and Rogers (1987), who examined the use of fear appeals to convince women to perform breast self-examinations in order to prevent the development of breast cancer.

As noted earlier, two versions of the sunscreen advertisement developed for the pre-test were used. The high threat advertisement contained vivid descriptions of skin cancer and its consequences (severity of threat) and emphasized the susceptibility of college students to it (probability of occurrence). The low threat commercial described skin cancer as a less severe illness with few consequences and emphasized its rarity among college students. Both versions of the advertisement then presented the new product as a way to prevent development of the disease.

Dependent Variables. Fear arousal was measured using Maddux and Rogers' (1983) six mood adjectives: frightened, tense, nervous, anxious, uncomfortable, and nauseous. Also, five items that Rippetoe and Rogers (1987) subsequently added to their scale to prevent respondents' guessing the underlying concept being measured were also utilized. Subjects rated the extent to which each adjective characterized their current state on a 9-point Likert-type scale ("not at all" to "very much"). Responses were then summed to produce a single index of fear for each subject.

Coping response was measured using McCrae's (1984) and Rippetoe and Rogers' (1987) operationalization. McCrae's (1984) findings indicated that when faced with a threat, individuals are more likely to use *fatalism* and *wishful thinking* as coping responses. In addition to these two maladaptive responses, consistent with the work of Rippetoe and Rogers (1987), *avoidance* and *hopelessness* were included due to their appropriateness as a response to a health threat. Thus, the present scale is composed of four distinct maladaptive coping responses. Likert-type items (7-point scale) were used for each coping response, and a mean score was calculated (Rippetoe and Rogers 1987).

Behavioral intention was operationalized as the intention to purchase the product described in the advertisement. Purchase intention was measured using three seven-point items anchored by very likely/very unlikely, probable/improbable, and possible/impossible. The scale, taken from Yi (1990), has been used in other consumer-related research (Lacher and Mizerki 1994, Lafferty and Goldsmith 1999).

Covariates. Three specific characteristics of an individual have been found to alter the relationship between fear and persuasion. According to Zuckerman (1978), *sensation seeking* refers to individuals' varying need for arousal. High sensation seekers have been found to be unconvinced by a high threat message (Witte and Morrison 1995), whereas low sensation seekers are more easily influenced (Schoenbachler and Whittler 1996). To assess sensation seeking, a shorter version of Zuckerman's (1978) Sensation Seeking Scale was administered to subjects (Madsen et al. 1987).

Self-esteem is another factor that has been found to affect the persuasive process of an advertisement using fear appeals. In fact, past research has indicated that compared to low self-esteem individuals, high self-esteem subjects manifest increased behavioral intention with increases in fear (Ramirez and Lasater 1977). To measure this variable, subjects completed Rosenberg's Self-Esteem Scale (1965).

Although sunscreen is a commonly used product, some people might not be in the habit of putting on lotion prior to exposure to the sun. The extent to which individuals use sunscreen could influence their intention to buy the product. Items designed to measure *product usage* were thus employed to control for individual differences. A three-item, seven-point, Likert-type scale was developed by the author to assess the frequency of sunscreen usage.

ANALYSIS AND RESULTS

Manipulation Checks

To assess the effectiveness of threat manipulation, two different scales (Rippetoe and Rogers 1987) were used: a four-item scale for *perceived severity* of skin cancer and a three-item scale for *probability of occurrence* of the disease. One-way ANOVA was performed to examine whether subjects' responses on these two scales varied across conditions (high vs. low threat). A successful manipulation would mean high scores on both the severity and the probability of occurrence scales for respondents in the high threat condition and low scores for those in the low threat group.

For the severity scale, a significant difference in the correct direction was found between the high and the low threat conditions ($\bar{x}_{low} = 4.33$, $\bar{x}_{high} = 4.91$, $F_{1,192} = 10.05$, $p < .002$), thus indicating an effective manipulation. No statistically significant result ($p > .05$), however, was obtained on the probability of occurrence manipulation (using either ANOVA or MANOVA procedures), thereby suggesting that this manipulation was not effective. Thus, one of the two fear components demonstrated a successful manipulation.

Relationships Between Covariates and Dependent Variables

Pearson correlations were computed to determine whether the proposed covariates (sensation seeking, self-esteem, and usage, as well as the demographic covariates age, gender, and year in school) were associated with the dependent variables. The results indicated that self-esteem, usage of sunscreen, and year in school were significantly correlated ($p < .05$) with at least one dependent variable. Consequently, these three variables were used in subsequent analyses. Sensation seeking, age, and gender, however, were not included, owing to their statistical insignificance ($p > .05$) with the dependent variables.

Hypothesis Test Results

A two-way MANCOVA was employed to test most of the hypotheses. Cronbach's alpha for all the measures exceeded 0.70. Table 1a presents the mean values for the dependent variables: fear, maladaptive coping, and purchase intention. Findings for MANCOVA appear in Table 1b.

H_1 predicted that a high level of threat would induce more fear than a low level of threat. Consistent with the hypothesis, the MANCOVA

TABLE 1a. Mean Values for Fear, Maladaptive Coping, and Purchase Intention

Dependent Variables	Level of Threat		Culture	
	Low	High	United States	France
Fear	2.71	3.52	3.12	3.11
Maladaptive Coping	3.27	3.17	3.09	3.37
Purchase Intention	3.51	3.95	3.80	3.66

TABLE 1b. MANCOVA Results for Relationships with Fear

Source	Wilk's Lambda	F	Hypothesis df	Error df	Significance
Threat	.92	5.57	3	185	<.01
Culture	.94	3.89	3	185	.01
Threat × Culture	.98	1.37	3	185	.25

generated a statistically significant main effect for the level of threat ($\Lambda = .92$, $F_{1,185} = 5.57$, $p < .01$). Univariate results revealed that the higher the level of threat, the greater the fear ($\bar{x}_{low} = 2.71$, $\bar{x}_{high} = 3.52$, $F_{1,187} = 13.01$, $p < .001$), thus lending support to H_1.

Hypothesis 2 proposed that fear would be negatively related to maladaptive coping, while Hypothesis 3 posited that there would be a negative relationship between maladaptive coping and purchase intention. Regression analysis results (Table 2a) indicated that fear is not a significant predictor of maladaptive coping ($p > .05$). Consequently, there is no support for Hypothesis 2. Similarly, as illustrated in Table 2b, there is no significant relationship between maladaptive coping and purchase intention ($p > .05$); so, H3 is rejected.

The fourth and the fifth hypotheses pertained to the effect of culture on fear and maladaptive coping, respectively. It was predicted that at a high level of threat, people from high uncertainty avoidance countries would report lower levels of fear (H_4) and generate more maladaptive coping responses (H_5) than individuals from low uncertainty avoidance cultures. Because the two-way interaction effect between level of threat and culture was not statistically significant (Table 1b; $\Lambda = .98$, $F_{3,185} = 1.37$, $p > .05$), neither H_4 nor H_5 is supported. Nonetheless, univariate results showed that the pattern of interaction was consistent with the prediction for maladaptive coping (see Figure 2).

TABLE 2a. Regression Results for Fear Predicting Maladaptive Coping

Variable	Unstandardized Coefficient		Std. Coefficient		
	B	SE	β	t	Sig.
Fear	.083	.048	.125	1.736	.085
Self-esteem	−.120	.172	−.050	−.693	.489
Use	−.091	.040	−.165	−2.284	.023
Year in School	−.001	.106	−.0008	−.012	.991

$R^2 = .043$, $F_{4,189} = 2.118$, $p > .082$

TABLE 2b. Regression Results for Maladaptive Coping Predicting Purchase Intention

Variable	Unstandardized Coefficient		Std. Coefficient		
	B	SE	β	t	Sig.
Maladaptive Coping	.017	.097	.013	.179	.858
Self-esteem	−.293	.230	−.090	−1.296	.205
Use	.190	.054	.250	3.514	<.001
Year in School	−.221	.142	−.108	−1.552	.122

$R^2 = .091$, $F_{4, 187} = 4.734$, $p < .001$

Post-Hoc Analysis

As discussed earlier, adaptive coping has not been found to be related to fear in past research. Given that this study's maladaptive coping findings were not significant, and thus not supportive of the hypotheses, relationships between fear and adaptive coping, as well as between adaptive coping and purchase intention, were examined. Identical analyses to those conducted for the maladaptive coping variable were performed. Moreover, MANCOVA was performed to test for main and interaction effects with adaptive coping as a dependent variable.

Mean values for the main effects of the independent variable (level of threat) and the blocking variable (culture) on adaptive coping are reported in Table 3a. In addition, results from the MANCOVA analysis are shown in Table 3b. A statistically significant main effect for level of threat was found ($\Lambda = .93$, $F_{3, 184} = 4.97$, $p < .01$). Univariate results indicated that there was a main effect for the level of threat on fear ($F_{1, 186} =$

FIGURE 2. The Interaction Effect of Uncertainty Avoidance and Level of Threat on Maladaptive Coping

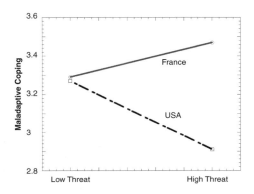

13.01, p < .001) and on purchase intention ($F_{1, 186}$ = 4.86, p < .05), but not on adaptive coping ($F_{1, 186}$ = 1.95, p > .16). Furthermore, MANCOVA generated a significant interaction effect between threat and culture (Λ = .95, $F_{3, 184}$ = 3.23, p < .05). Univariate findings showed a significant interaction effect between threat and culture for adaptive coping ($F_{1, 186}$ = 9.77, p < .002), but not for fear ($F_{1, 186}$ = 1.11, p > .29), nor for purchase intention ($F_{1, 186}$ = .23, p > .63).

The relationships between fear and adaptive coping as well as between adaptive coping and purchase intention were investigated using regression analyses (Table 3c). Fear was found to be positively related to adaptive coping (β = .355, t = 5.261, p < .001), and adaptive coping was significantly and positively associated with purchase intention (β = .287, t = 4.128, p < .001). Because these two relationships were statistically significant, the relationship between fear and purchase intention was tested. Given that the findings revealed that fear was a significant predictor of purchase intention (β = .283, t = 4.082, p < .001), a fourth regression was conducted to test for the mediation effect of adaptive coping (which is consistent with the proposed effect of the maladaptive coping variable illustrated in Figure 1). Baron and Kenny (1986) suggest that mediation is present if the effect of the independent variable on the dependent variable is reduced when the mediator is entered in the equation. Consistent with this condition, when the influence of fear and adaptive coping on purchase intention was examined, the fear coefficient value was smaller (β = .207, t = 2.855, p < .001) relative to the one obtained in

TABLE 3a. Mean Values for Adaptive Coping

Dependent Variable	Level of Threat		Culture	
	Low	High	United States	France
Adaptive Coping	4.29	4.54	4.33	4.50

TABLE 3b. MANCOVA Results for Fear, Adaptive Coping, and Purchase Intention

Source	Wilk's Lambda	F	Hypothesis df	Error df	Significance
Threat	.93	4.97	3	184	<.01
Culture	.97	1.95	3	184	.12
Threat × Culture	.95	3.23	3	184	.02

TABLE 3c. Regression Analysis Results for Mediation Effect of Adaptive Coping

Regression	Independent Variable(s)	Dependent Variable	β	p-value	R^2	$F_{1,192}$	p-value
1	Fear	Adaptive Coping	.355	.000	.126	27.681	<.001
2	Adaptive Coping	Purchase Intention	.286	.000	.082	17.041	<.001
3	Fear	Purchase Intention	.283	.000	.080	16.666	<.001
4	Fear Adaptive Coping	Purchase Intention	.207 .212	.005 .004	.119	12.913	<.001

the third regression. Therefore, this demonstrates that adaptive coping mediates the relationship between fear and purchase intention.

DISCUSSION AND IMPLICATIONS

Effect of Threat

Consistent with the hypothesis, a high level of threat induced more fear than a low level. This is compatible with a basic tenet of protection motivation theory (Rogers 1983). The few advertising studies using the protection motivation theory as their basic framework (e.g., Schoen-bachler and Whittler 1996; Tanner et al. 1991) have been mostly concerned about consumers' intentions to adopt a healthy behavior (e.g., usage of a condom). The focus in the present work, though, was on buying intentions for a specific health-related *product*. Therefore, this study makes a contribution to the literature of fear appeals in advertising owing to its focus on product-, rather than idea-related, advertising.

Effect of Culture

Cultures high in uncertainty avoidance were proposed to be less fearful relative to those that are low in uncertainty avoidance. In other words, in a high threat condition, French people were hypothesized to be less fearful than their American counterparts; no significant difference, though, was obtained. This prediction was based on Hofstede's (1980) work on cultural dimensions. Because Hofstede collected his data nearly three decades ago, his classification could be less appropriate now. Indeed, national characteristics are subject to change as political, economic, and social changes shape society (Fernandez, Carlson, Stepina, and Nicholson, 1997). Consequently, France and U.S. values may be more compatible today than at the time of Hofstede's study; thus, consumers from both countries may display similar reactions to a fear-inducing persuasive message.

On the other hand, the nature of the threat, as well as the subjects' age group, could account for the non-significant findings. In fact, U.S. college students frequently expose themselves to ultra-violet rays without excessively worrying about the consequences. A vivid example is the popularity of tanning salons in the region where the study was conducted. Consequently, the skin cancer threat possibly was not as potent a threat as expected for the U.S. respondents in the current study.

Interestingly, although the results were not statistically significant, the interaction between threat and culture on maladaptive coping supported the prediction: At a high level of threat, French consumers exhibited more maladaptive coping than American participants. In light of these findings, the impact of nationality could work directly at the coping stage instead of influencing fear, as previously hypothesized. In other words, even though no difference emerged in the expression of fear, people from the two countries under study seemed to cope with the threat using distinctly different approaches.

Relationships Between the Dependent Variables

Fear was expected to have a negative effect on maladaptive coping, which was subsequently supposed to be negatively related to purchase intention. Although these predictions were developed based on an established model in the field of fear appeals, no statistical support was found. As discussed earlier, a mediation effect of maladaptive, and not adaptive coping, has been demonstrated in past health-promotion research (e.g., Ho 2000; Rippetoe and Rogers 1987).

One possible explanation for the unexpected outcome in the current study may be the content of the persuasive message used in the experiment. If the fear-arousing message had outlined the ineffectiveness of maladaptive coping modes in overcoming the threat, conceivably, maladaptive coping could play a mediating role in the relationship between fear and behavioral intention. However, in the context of the present study, owing to the limited space in a print advertisement, only the threat, followed by an *adaptive* behavior (buying the advertised sunscreen), were presented. Consequently, the readers were not led to focus on the maladaptive coping responses.

The influence of fear on adaptive coping and the impact of adaptive coping on purchase intention were explored. The results showed that fear was positively related to adaptive coping, which, in turn, had a positive effect on purchase intention. A test of the mediating effect of adaptive coping was also conclusive. Therefore, these findings suggest that the nature of the mediator could vary according to the content of the persuasive message. Likewise, examining adaptive coping instead of maladaptive coping in the context of advertising may be particularly appropriate.

Implications

The findings of this research suggest several theoretical, as well as managerial, implications. Although challenging previous studies, the mediation effect of adaptive coping demonstrated in this study represents a contribution to the protection motivation theory literature. Researchers should not assume that maladaptive coping is necessarily the mediator involved. As discussed above, if the persuasive message does not highlight the inadequacy of maladaptive coping, there is no reason to believe that this would be a crucial variable influencing the relationship between fear and purchase intention.

Despite the fact that some studies have previously applied the protection motivation model in the advertising field, none has examined the purchase intention of a specific product. In fact, prior studies were mostly concerned about using fear appeals in an advertisement to predict the intention to perform a healthy behavior. Therefore, the influence of the level of threat on purchase intention found in this study constitutes additional support for the applicability of protection motivation theory in the marketing domain.

This latter finding also has implications for advertising practitioners. If properly used, fear appeals can prompt consumers to buy the advertised product. However, before launching an advertising campaign presenting some kind of threat, marketers should conduct research to determine whether this strategy is suitable for their target audience as well as the product type.

Although cross-cultural research has often emphasized the importance of adopting different advertising strategies according to the target country, the results of this study indicate that fear appeals seem to be effective in both France and the United States when the communication is directed at young people for health-related products. This standardization would represent tremendous cost reductions for practitioners interested in marketing their product in either country.

Limitations and Future Research

Some limitations of this study emerge from the control of variables that an experiment setting makes possible. Because control of internal validity was a primary concern, the external validity of the findings may be somewhat affected. In fact, when exposed to an advertisement in an actual context, people might not pay as much attention as when they are asked to evaluate one specific advertisement. Moreover, the absence of articles in a magazine or of other advertisements does not reflect reality. Future studies should attempt to place the ad in a short version of a magazine, for instance.

As discussed above, level of threat was manipulated according to the severity of the threat and the subject's probability of occurrence of the threat (vulnerability). The results of the manipulation checks, however, indicated significant differences for severity across the two conditions, but not for vulnerability.

Although some potential confounding factors were included in the analysis, others should be considered in future research, such as the amount of prior knowledge about the threat. An attempt was made, in the pretest, to create fictitious scenarios to remove any extraneous influence of knowledge, but subjects appeared to be skeptical of the contrived situations. Research effort should be directed at exploring the fear induced by novel threats. Similarly, respondents' perceptions of the skin cancer threat may have been muted owing to political unrest the western world is currently experiencing.

In addition, the findings of this study are restricted to the student population, specific target product, and print advertisements. As mentioned earlier, young people might be less fearful and less health conscious than other age groups. Research should attempt to replicate the results with different populations and other types of products. Since fear appeals have been mostly examined in the health-promotion context, empirical effort is needed to determine whether fear could influence the purchase intention of hedonic products, for example. The effectiveness of fear appeals in other types of media should also be investigated.

Findings of the present research indicated that adaptive coping (and not maladaptive coping) was a mediator between fear and purchase intention, which does not support results in past studies. One explanation advanced to account for this result is concerned with the extent to which the persuasive message emphasizes the ineffectiveness of maladaptive coping. This represents an interesting avenue for future research. Despite the fact that no significant differences in fear were found between French and U.S. consumers, valuable information was gained from these results. An important direction for future research is exploring the application of fear appeals, and more specifically, the protection motivation model in other cross-cultural settings. Finally, this study focuses on the fear induced by the advertisement itself rather than fear generated by the context (i.e., by a television program in which a commercial could be embedded). Future studies should investigate this promising line of research.

REFERENCES

Arnold, V. D. (1985), "The Importance of Pathos in Persuasive Appeals," *The Bulletin*, 26-27.

Assael, Henry (1995), *Consumer Behavior and Marketing Action*. Cincinnati, OH: Southwestern College Publishing.

Barron, R. M., and D. A. Kenny (1986), "The Moderator-Mediator Variable Distinction in Social Psychological Research: Conceptual, Strategic, and Statistical Considerations," *Journal of Personality and Social Psychology*, 51, 1173-1182.

Biswas, A., J. E. Olsen, and V. Carlet (1992), "A Comparison of Print Advertisements from the United States and France," *Journal of Advertising*, 21, 73-81.

Boster, F. J., and P. Mongeau (1984), "Fear-arousing Persuasive Messages," In *Communication Yearbook*, Vol. 8, R. Bostrom, ed., Newbury Park, CA: Sage, 330-375.

Breckler, S. J. (1993), "Emotion and Attitude Change," In *Handbook of Emotions*, M. Lewis and J. M. Haviland, eds., New York: Guilford Press, 461-473.

Chinese Culture Connection (1987), "Chinese Values and the Search for Culture-free Dimensions of Culture," *Journal of Cross-Cultural Psychology*, 18 (2), 143-164.

Fredrikson, M., P. Annas and H. Fischer (1996), "Gender and Age Differences in the Prevalence of Specific Fears and Phobias," *Behavior Research and Therapy*, 34, 33-39.

Girandola, F. (2000), "Fear and Persuasion: Review and Reanalysis of the Literature (1953-1998)," *L'Année Psychologique*, 100, 333-376.

Gudykunst, W. B. and S. Ting-Toomey (1988), "Culture and Affective Communication," *American Behaviorial Scientist*, 31, 384-400.

Higbee, K. L. (1969), "Fifteen Years of Fear Arousal: Research on Threat Appeals 1953-1968," *Psychological Bulletin*, 72, 426-444.

Ho, R. (2000), "Predicting Intention for Protective Health Behavior: A Test of the Protection Versus the Ordered Protection Motivation Model," *Australian Journal of Psychology*, 52, 110-118.

Hofstede, G. (1980), *Culture's Consequences: International Differences in Work-Related Values*, Beverly Hills, CA: Sage Publications.

Hofstede, G. (1991), *Cultures and Organizations: Software of the Mind*, London: McGraw-Hill.

Izard, C. E. (1971), *The Face of Emotions*, New York: Appleton-Century-Crofts.

Janis, I. L. (1967), "Effects of fear arousal on attitude change: Recent developments in theory and experimental research." In L. Berkowitz (Ed.), *Advances in Experimental Social Psychology*, Vol. 3 (pp. 166-224). New York: University Press.

Janis, I. L., and Fesbach, S. (1953), Effects of fear-arousing communications. *Journal of Abnormal and Social Psychology*, 48, 78-92.

Janis, I. L., and H. Leventhal (1968), "Human Reactions to Stress," In *Handbook of Personality and Research*, E. Borgotta, and W. Lambert, eds., (1041-1085). Chicago: Rand McNally.

Janis, I. L., and R. F. Terwilliger (1962), "An Experimental Study of Psychological Resistances to Fear-Arousing Communications," *Journal of Abnormal and Social Psychology*, 65, 403-410.

Lacher, K. T., and R. Mizerski (1994), "An Exploratory Study of the Responses and Relationships Involved in the Evaluation of, and in the Intention to Purchase New Rock Music," *Journal of Consumer Research*, 21, 366-381.

Lafferty, B. A., and R. E. Goldsmith (1999), "Corporate Credibility Role's in Consumers' Attitudes and Purchase Intentions When a High Versus a Low Credibility Endorser is Used in the Ad," *Journal of Business Research*, 44, 109-116.

LaTour, M. S. and R. E. Pitts (1989), "Using Fear Appeals In Advertising For AIDS Prevention In The College-Age Population," *Journal of Health Care Marketing*, 9, 5-14.

LaTour, M. S., R. L. Snipes, and S. J. Bliss (1996), "Don't Be Afraid to Use Fear Appeals: An Experimental Study," *Journal of Advertising Research*, 36, 59-67.

Lavack, A. M. (1997), Fear Appeals in Social Marketing Advertising, Unpublished doctoral dissertation, University of British Columbia, Canada.

Lustig, M. W. and J. Koester (1998), *Intercultural Competence: Interpersonal Communication Across Cultures*, New York: Addison Wesley Longman.

Lynn, R. (1975), "National Differences in Anxiety." In *Stress and Anxiety*, I. G. Sarason and C. D. Spielberger, eds., Washington, DC: Hemisphere, 153-167.

Maddux, J. E., and R. W. Rogers (1983), "Protection Motivation and Self-Efficacy: A Revised Theory of Fear Appeals and Attitude Change," *Journal of Experimental Social Psychology*, 19, 469-479.

Madsen, D. B., A. K. Das, I. Bogen, and E. E. Grossman (1987), "A Short Sensation-Seeking Scale," *Psychological Reports*, 60, 1179-1184.

Maheswaran, D. and S. Shavitt (2000), "Issues and New Directions in Global Consumer Psychology," *Journal of Consumer Psychology*, 9, 59-66.

Matsumoto, D. (1989), "Cultural Influences on the Perception of Emotion," *Journal of Cross-Cultural Psychology*, 20, 92-105.

McCrae, R. R. (1984), "Situational Determinants of Coping Responses: Loss, Threat, and Challenge," *Journal of Personality and Social Psychology*, 46, 919-928.

Ramirez, A., and T. M. Lasater (1977), "Ethnicity of Communicators, Self-Esteem, and Reactions to Fear-Arousing Communications," *Journal of Social Psychology*, 102, 79-91.

Rippetoe, P. A., and R. W. Rogers (1987), "Effects of Components of Protection Motivation Theory on Adaptive and Maladaptive Coping with a Health Threat," *Journal of Personality and Social Psychology*, 52, 596-604.

Rogers, R. W. (1983), "Cognitive and Physiological Processes in Fear Appeals and Attitude Change: A Revised Theory of Protection Motivation." In *Social Psychophysiology*, J. Cacioppo and R. Petty, eds., New York: Guilford Press, 153-176.

Rosenberg, M. (1965), *Society and the Adolescent Self-Image*, Princeton, NJ: Prentice-Hall.

Schimmack, U. (1996), "Cultural Influences on the Recognition of Emotion by Facial Expressions: Individualistic or Caucasian Cultures?", *Journal of Cross-Cultural Psychology*, 27, 37-50.

Schoenbachler, D. D., and T. E. Whittler (1996), "Adolescent Processing of Social and Physical Threat Communications," *Journal of Advertising*, 25, 37-54.

Sutton, S. R. (1982), "Fear Arousing Communications: A Critical Examination of Theory and Research," In *Social Psychology and Behavioral Medicine*, J. R. Eiser, ed., New York: John Wiley and Sons, 303-338.

Tanner, J. F., J. B. Hunt and D. R. Eppright (1991), "The Protection Motivation Model: A Normative Model of Fear Appeals," *Journal of Marketing*, 55, 36-45.

Taylor, C. R. and B. B. Stern (1997), "Asian-Americans: Television Advertising and the 'Model Minority' Stereotype," *Journal of Advertising*, 26, 47-61.

Toyne, B. and P. G. Walters (1993), "Global Marketing Management," Needam Heights, MA: Allyn and Bacon.

Van de Vijver, F. and K. Leung (1997), "Methods and Data Analysis of Comparative Research," In *Handbook of Cross-Cultural Psychology: Vol. 1 Theory and Method*,

J. W. Berry, Y. H. Poortinga and J. Pandey, eds., Needham Heights, MA: Allyn and Bacon, 257-300.

Wallbott, H. G., P. Ricci-Bitti, and E. Banninger-Huber (1986), "Non-Verbal Reactions to Emotional Experiences," In *Experiencing Emotions: A Cross-Cultural Study*, K. Scherer, H. G. Wallbott, and A. B. Summerfield, eds., Cambridge, UK: Cambridge University Press, 69-83.

Wallbott, H. G. and K. R. Scherer (1986), "The Antecedents of Emotional Experiences," In *Experiencing Emotions: A Cross-Cultural Study*, K. Scherer, H. G. Wallbott, and A. B. Summerfield, eds., Cambridge, UK: Cambridge University Press.

Witte, K. and K. Morrison (1995), "Using Scare Tactics to Promote Safe Sex Among Juvenile Detention and High School Youth," *Journal of Applied Communication Research*, 23, 128-142.

Yi, Y. (1990), "Cognitive and Affective Priming Effects of the Context for Print Advertisements," *Journal of Advertising*, 19, 40-48.

Zuckerman, M. (1978), *Sensation Seeking: Beyond the Optimal Level of Arousal*, Hillsdale, NJ: Lawrence Erlbaum Associates.

Index